Another Kind of Rebel

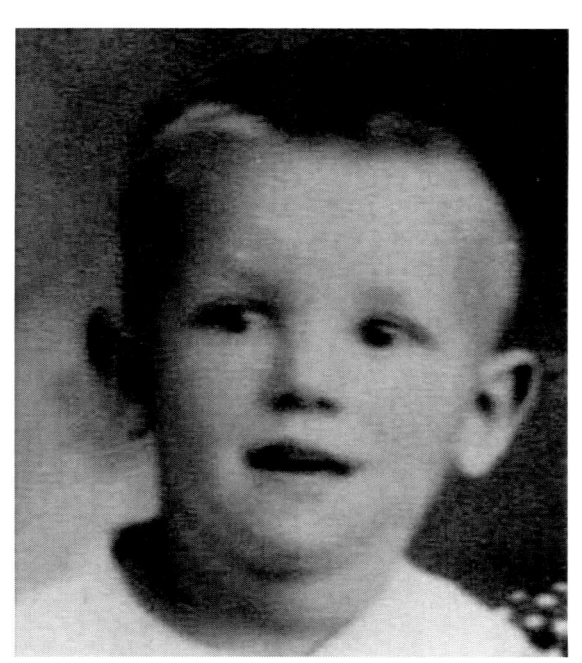

To Liz & Greg
from Olivia

A Memoir by Robert Thomason

Check out pages 51, 55, 68 & 168
My dear friend of many years

Copyright © 2020 by Robert T. Thomason
All rights reserved.

Second Printing

Published by:

Robert T. Thomason
19 Tulipwood Court Unit A
St. Johns, Florida 32259
(386) 503-4683
thomasonrobt@gmail.com

ISBN 978-1-64999-393-9

Cover Design Suggested by Alaina Thomason

Table of Contents

Foreword 1

Part I   The Early Years 3

My Roots 3

My Nuclear Family 4

My Extended Family 6

My Segregated Society 7

My Childhood "Innocence" 8

The Boy Scouts 9

Jews and Racism 11

My Civil War Education 14

The Church in the Center 16

Waking Up 17

Part II   The College and Law School Years 18

My Freshman Year 18

The North Georgia Conference Methodist Youth Fellowship 19

A Lake Junaluska Experience 21

National Gatherings at Purdue University 22

The Georgia United Christian Youth Movement 24

Finding My Soulmate 26

An Experience at Brevard and Oxford 27

General Board of Social and Economic Relations 28

The Central Jurisdiction 31

Part III   The Law Years 35

In the Middle District of Georgia 35

Integration of the University of Georgia 37

Voting Rights in Terrell County 40

Koinonia Farm and the Americus School Board 42

Taking a Different Road 46

Part IV   Seminary and Ordination 48

The Seminary Years 48

Ordination 53

Part V   LaGrange and Oakwood 54

Ma Barton and the Barton Trust 54

LaGrange 55

The Help 56

LaGrange Council on Human Relations 57

Oakwood 65

Part VI Milledgeville 69

Weekly Recreation Program for State Hospital Patients 73

Concern 74

School Lunches 76

Black History 80

Voter Registration 80

Peonage 81

Two More "Revelations" 81

A Disturbing Conversation 83

Tutoring Program 84

Flannery O'Connor 87

Family Matters 89

Head Start 90

PTA Luncheon 91

The Barton Trust: Neil Jen 91

The Barton Trust: Lucretia Coleman 92

The Funeral of Dr. Martin Luther King, Jr. 95

An Interracial Romance 97

Church Politics 98

A Tribute to Charles Alston   100

Part VII   Emory University   101

Moving On   101

Emory University, Again   102

Seminars on White Racism   103

Koinonia Farm   106

Southeastern Campus Ministers Conferences   107

A Sunday in April   108

Summer Vocational Intern Program (SVIP)   110

North Georgia Methodists for Church Renewal   111

A Trip with Maurice Cherry   114

The Anti-War and the Women's Movements   115

The Barton Trust: Christopher Egwim   116

More Family Matters   119

A Visit in Santa Fe with Sister Carmen   120

Metro Atlanta Higher Education Ministry (MAHEM)   122

Part VIII   Jacksonville   123

A New Start   123

Jacksonville Campus Ministry   126

Edward Waters College   128

Florida Junior College, Downtown   129

Christmas International House   130

A Sermon at Arlington Presbyterian Church   131

Methodist Federation for Social Action   132

Jacksonville Clergy for Alternatives to the Death Penalty   133

Part IX   Northern Virginia   136

Conferences and Consultations   136

United College Ministries in Northern Virginia   138

Multiracial, Multicultural Staffing   139

Apartheid in South Africa   141

Virginia Campus Ministry Forum   142

More Family Matters   143

Betty Williams Perkins   145

An Evening with Toni Morrison   146

Victoria Gray Adams   147

Building Our Dream House   149

More Family Matters   150

Part X   The Retirement Years   152

The Big "C"   152

National Campus Ministry Association (NCMA)   153

Palm Coast United Methodist Church   154

Heavenly Hospitality   156

More Family Matters   156

Joy in the Morning   159

Publications   160

Male-Female Relationships   161

Memorial Presbyterian Church   163

Church Committee on Racial Reconciliation   165

Seekers   167

Feeding Homeless People   167

Methodist Federation for Social Action, Again   169

Travel   170

Martin Luther King Holiday Breakfasts   171

Crossing in St. Augustine   172

More Family Matters and the Big "C"   173

Part XI   Westminster Woods on Julington Creek   174

More Travel   175

Life at Westminster   176

The Big "C" Again—and Again   177

Lots of Reunions   178

Lunch at the South Beach Grill   179

A Special Note About Betty   181

More Family Matters   181

The Big "S"   183

Part XII   Ancestry   183

My Ancestors and Indian Lands   184

My Ancestors and Slave Ownership   184

My Ancestors and the Civil War   187

Lynching   189

Part XIII   The Future   191

Reparations, Monuments, and Systemic Racism   191

Some Books About Race That Have Changed My Life   192

Planning My Future   194

Afterword   197

Foreword

I would probably never have written this memoir if two events had not occurred simultaneously. First, George Perry Floyd was murdered on May 25, 2020, by Minneapolis police officers in a brutal manner--having his breath extinguished by holding him face down on the pavement with a knee on his neck for eight minutes and forty-six seconds. Mr. Floyd's death felt like the "last straw" in my lifetime of witnessing unspeakable racist acts in the land of my birth.

Second, at the time of Mr. Floyd's murder and for many weeks afterwards (total number yet to be determined), I have largely been confined to my home at Westminster Woods on Julington Creek to avoid becoming infected with the coronavirus Covid-19. That unique experience has given me ample time to reflect on my life in the South and to search for a deeper understanding of the many ways the plague of racism has shaped the person I am and the life I have lived.

I have chosen to tell my story chronologically through a series of vignettes, telling stories about significant life events that have taught me about the insidious nature and scope of racism. Some of my story has already been told in a memoir written largely by my late wife Rose before her death in 2001. As she was writing, she would often give me her account of something we had both experienced for me to read. If I said, "Well, that's not exactly how I remember it," she would answer, "This is my story; you write yours." So, Rose, after many years of procrastination, here it is.

I hope there will be those who want to read it. If so, I am pleased to share it, "warts and all." I particularly hope my two sons, daughter-in-law, grandson, and six granddaughters will want to read it. Whether they realize it or not, these experiences have helped to shape the persons they are.

The title I chose reflects two aspects of the person I am. First, by birth, I am a "white boy," with deep roots in the South, whose DNA derives from slaveholders, Confederate rebel soldiers as well as Union sympathizers, and inheritors of stolen Cherokee land, one whose entire life has been lived in the former Confederate states. Second, by choice, I am a rebel against the status quo, one who, as Rose described it, was gifted with a passion for justice, and with the courage, sometimes, to follow that passion.

I have never been particularly introspective, but one cannot understand racism in oneself and in society without doing much soul-searching. Just a month short of my 85th birthday as I began this, I thought my greatest challenge would be remembering events and details. That has not been the case. Rather, I learned that understanding the feelings generated by the memories and being willing to confront and share them posed a greater challenge. What follows is my best effort to tell my story with honesty and candor. I hope that, in doing so, my story might help those who read it better understand their stories.

Part I   The Early Years

My Roots

I grew up in the northwest corner of Georgia, in the small textile town of Dalton, county seat of Whitfield County. Dalton is in a wide valley, with the Appalachian Plateau on the west and the Blue Ridge Mountains on the east. It borders Tennessee on the north and is only one county away from Alabama on the west. In the years of my childhood (1935-53), a major railroad ran through the middle of town, connecting Atlanta (90 miles south) to Chattanooga (30 miles north). A major north/south highway, U.S. 41, skirted downtown by two blocks. My family's home was directly on Highway 41, called Dixie Highway, three blocks from the railroad and almost a mile from downtown.

Our county was named for George Whitefield, early Georgia leader and revival preacher. At the time of his death, he owned 75 slaves. Here is what he thought of slavery: "Though liberty is a sweet thing to such as are born free, yet to those who never knew the sweets of it, slavery may perhaps not be so irksome." He goes on to say that "hot countries cannot be cultivated without negroes," and that it's too bad the colony of Georgia hadn't approved slavery before then, because "how many white people have been destroyed for want of them, and how many thousands of pounds spent to no purpose of all?"

This, too, is a part of my heritage.

My Nuclear Family

My father, Albert Troy (called Troy) Thomason, completed the seventh grade in his rural public school in Tilton, on the railroad ten miles from town. It was all the education available unless you could travel to Dalton. His two older brothers had gone to Akron, Ohio, to work in the tire factory. Before he was 21, he joined them there. To finance his move, he made rabbit boxes, in which he trapped and sold wild rabbits.

In the early 30s, when they had accumulated enough money, the brothers returned to Dalton, where they opened a café in downtown. It had one long counter with stools, and provided curb service on metal trays. Their specialty was a huge, ten-cent hamburger. They were open from 6:00 a.m. to midnight.

Even though it was the Depression, my dad and his brother Clarence made enough money to purchase a dry goods store in the next block sometime in the late 30s. The brothers soon had a "falling out," the nature of which I could never learn. My dad purchased his brother's interest, and they never spoke directly to one another for the rest of their lives, although they would sit in the same room at their parents' home.

After finishing elementary school, my mother, Louie Ruth Roach (called Louie), was able to go to high school in Dalton because her older brother had a car. When he graduated, she was still a year from getting her diploma. However, her sister Flossye had married and moved to Chattanooga. Mother went to live with her and completed high school at nearby Central High School. She came back home and taught in the Griffin School near Mill Creek. (Griffin was her mother's family name; I imagine most of the children in the school were part of her extended family.) It was a one-room schoolhouse divided by a curtain. She taught half the children at one end, and her cousin, Ovelle Masters, taught the other half. She "trained" for a summer at Georgia State College for Women in Milledgeville, either before or after she had started teaching.

My parents were married in 1933, and my sister Helen was born ten months later. I came along seventeen months after that, completing our family circle.

Helen was born with spina bifida. Our parents were told she would not live to be more than six. Consequently, she was never sent to public school but taught at home by my mother (and by me, after coming home in the afternoon). Today, she would have been mainstreamed and grown up to be a normal adult with handicapping conditions. Back then, she was reared in a protective environment, guarded from harm and humiliation. (She surprised everyone by living to age 82.)

In recent years I have begun to reflect on the impact having a severely handicapped sister has had on my life. As I mentioned above, I was one of her teachers. I was also one of her caregivers. A familiar refrain I remember throughout my childhood was "take care of your sister." I have come to see that my being both a teacher and a caregiver throughout my life is no happenstance but a fulfillment of roles I learned early in life.

My mother was a full-time mother and homemaker. However, she also "kept the books" for the store, assisted with buying, and worked in the store on Saturdays. I almost never saw her simply sitting down to relax. She had boundless energy, almost to the day she died.

My Extended Family

All of my forebears had come to northwest Georgia prior to the Civil War. Most were farmers who lived on subsistence farms in the rural areas of the county (or just across county borders in Walker, Gordon, or Chattooga County). Most had come soon after the Cherokee Indians, the natives of the area, were forced to move west on the infamous "Trail of Tears" in the late 1830s. Some received 160-acre lots directly from the lotteries that distributed Cherokee land.

All my grandparents (and one great-grandmother) lived in south Whitfield County on family farms. My mother had nine siblings; my dad, ten. Almost all of these aunts, uncles, and their children lived in the county. (I had thirty first cousins.) So I was part of a large local clan stretching back several generations.

While I was growing up, we took long Sunday afternoon drives around the rural parts of our county. We ended up, almost always, at the home of my Thomason grandparents on the Tilton-Carbondale Road. Many of my cousins would usually be there, too.

My mother was the middle child in her family—preceded by three older sisters and a brother, and followed by another brother and three younger sisters. (A third brother, the last child, died at age 6.) My mother's sisters and their families would usually gather at our house on holidays. Her three younger sisters were like three more mothers to Helen and me growing up, and their three sons were like our brothers. They were frequently in and out of our house.

My Segregated Society

The society of my childhood and youth was a thoroughly segregated one—separate (but unequal) schools, separate neighborhoods, separate churches. Most blacks (in "polite" circles we referred to them as "nigras") lived in an area just south of downtown in what was called "Black Bottom." It was bordered on the east by the railroad, and Mill Creek ran through it. This small stream always had a really bad smell. (Likely, there was no sewer system, and the stream carried away raw sewage.) The single black school (all grades), called the Emery Street School because of its location, was in the center of the community as was a church and a funeral home.

The S-Curve was an infamous traffic hazard on Highway 41 at a major intersection south of town. I suspect it was designed that way to accommodate an influential landowner. In town, the highway was called Thornton Avenue and, north of the S-Curve, it was a fashionable main thoroughfare with beautiful old homes (some antebellum) and towering old growth trees.

I lived in the first block south of the S-Curve, a less fashionable area but in a very nice brick house built by my parents when I was three or four years of age. Just beyond the houses on the east side of Thornton Avenue was Black Bottom. When I walked or rode my bike downtown, I always went north on Thornton Avenue, never going through Black Bottom, even though I could have saved a few steps by doing so. I'm sure I would have been safe, but it "just wasn't done." The only public building there, serving almost as a fence separating it from downtown, was the local jail.

Unlike much of middle and south Georgia, northwest Georgia was not plantation country, Consequently, the black population was not very large—certainly less than ten per cent. Growing up, almost the only place I encountered a person of color was downtown. My dad and mother owned and operated a small dry goods store, named Thomason & Co., located on the west side of Hamilton Street, the "main drag," as we called it. There were five blocks downtown, stretching north and south. In the middle were the post office, a multi-story hotel, and a bronze statue of Joseph E. Johnston, Confederate Civil War general and local hero, with the railroad depot a short half block east.

Our family's store was a block and a half south of there. Several of our customers were people of color. I was unaware of any discrimination in the way they were treated in the store. Of course, all of our employees were white. My dad extended credit to customers on a very personal basis, no credit checks involved. I know that several people of color, mostly women, were among his credit customers. I was also aware that he addressed some but not all of the women of color with the title Mrs., although that was not the local custom.

I worked in the store from a young age. Always smaller than my peers, I would sometimes be told by a customer, when I asked if I might help them, "No, you're too little."

My Childhood "Innocence"

Unlike many Southern children, I had no black playmates. The only two individual blacks I knew "personally" were employed by my mother's sister Ivan and her husband Willard. Mabel Macon worked as their domestic servant, attired in the appropriate uniform declaring her status. She helped care for their two children, cooked, and cleaned. Since I was often in their house, I spent many hours with her. Although careful never to step out of her subservient role, she was sometimes feisty. I liked being around her.

Gordon Willis worked primarily in my uncle's coal and feed business, but he often performed chores around their house as well and sometimes drove us places. He was a handsome man, always dressed neatly, and, in my memory, just like Hoke Colburn, the character played by Morgan Freeman in the film *Driving Miss Daisy*. (Throughout my lifetime, the Willis family has been "related" to my family. As recently as 2016, Gordon's grandson, Lamar Austin, tended to the lawn and needed repairs of my family's home in Dalton until the death of my sister, the final occupant.)

I don't recall ever hearing my parents use the N-word or speak in a derogatory way about blacks, although I certainly heard others, including members of my extended family, do so. I remember feeling uncomfortable when they did, like being around folks who were constantly using profanity. I don't recall ever witnessing overt mistreatment of blacks, although, in retrospect, I can't imagine that to be true.

The Boy Scouts

My first semi-awakening experience about race occurred when I was twelve or thirteen. The scouting program was a central part of my formative years. I had joined the Cub Scouts as soon as I was old enough (nine, I think), and became a real Boy Scout when I was twelve. My scoutmaster was Devine Hubbs. He was also my Sunday School teacher and became the most influential mentor of my youth. I almost "worshipped" him.

Largely because of him, I imagine, I continued to be an active scout until I graduated from high school, attaining the rank of Eagle and serving eventually as Junior Assistant Scoutmaster.

My first Camporee was held in the City Park adjacent to the County Courthouse. I remember two exciting activities that occurred. We built a tower by lashing logs together with ropes, and we cooked a meal in the ground by digging a hole, lining it with rocks, building a fire to heat the rocks, removing the fire, putting our food wrapped in leaves on the rocks, covering it, and letting it cook for hours. We called it imu.

Several other scout troops from our Cherokee District were also participating in the Camporee. Much to my surprise, one of them was a troop of black boys from Dalton. Their scoutmaster was the funeral director in the black community, and he and Mr. Hubbs appeared to be good friends. No one seemed upset about their presence, just astonished, since interracial social interaction was not the custom in Dalton. Most of our time, though, was spent with our own troop that weekend, and I recall little interaction with the black scouts. Still, I had never before been around black boys of my age, certainly not in a social setting of equality, and I began to wonder about racial separation.

The Boy Scouts also provided my first introduction to the world beyond Dalton. I grew up, of course, without television. My only window to the outside world was all the traffic that traveled on U.S. 41 in front of my house. (That highway was the equivalent of today's I-75, stretching from the Upper Peninsula of Michigan to Miami, Florida.) Being the curious kid I was, I jumped at the chance at age 14 to attend the

National Boy Scout Jamboree in Valley Forge, Pennsylvania, with side trips by train to Washington and Philadelphia.

When I was 17, I again took part in another National Boy Scout Jamboree in Irvine Ranch, California, traveling by train through the Rockies and across the Great Plains. There were probably 30,000 boys at each of these events from all across the country. I'm sure there must have been black scouts, but I recall no experience that penetrated my provincialism. Embarrassingly, I do remember that at Irvine Ranch my buddy and I displayed the Confederate battle flag on our hats. To me, at that time, it had nothing to do with the Civil War. It was just a mark of identification, the equivalent of wearing a catamount, the mascot of my high school. I had much to learn about the meaning of symbols and how hurtful they can be for others.

Jews and Racism

I have struggled with this question: Is prejudice/discrimination against Jews appropriately termed "racism"? While I don't know how scholars would answer, I know that it "feels" like racism.

A Jewish family, the Bravers, lived directly behind us throughout my childhood. Mr. Braver (Jack) was a merchant like my father. His dry goods store of a comparable size was a block south of my parents' store. Mrs. Braver (Helen) was a housewife, like my mother, who participated in the business as well. They had two daughters, Patsy and Betty, both younger than me. They also had an adult son (Bill), who married a Gentile and was "shunned" by his family until, a few years later, after their divorce, he was restored to the fold.

Our houses were separated by a six-foot-high hedge that, conveniently, had an opening one could walk through. Until we reached pre-adolescence, Patsy and Betty were daily playmates, almost always at our house. Our parents were not friends but were friendly toward one another.

Something happened when I was maybe ten years old that I found extremely distressing. Although my memory of this event is vague, my sense that it was momentous is clear. I can see the whole Braver family standing on the walkway just outside our back door. It is twilight, and my family is standing on our back porch, atop a few steps. There are angry voices, and I am being accused of some misbehavior involving either Patsy and/or Betty. I suspect it was of a sexual nature but don't really remember that. (I hardly knew the word "sex" at that age.) Whatever the incident was about, we seldom played together after that.

Growing up, I remember my father making what today I would deem anti-Semitic remarks. His store was on a block bordered by maybe ten other stores. Three of them were modest dry goods stores similar to his, all operated by Jewish merchants. My dad had determined, early on, what he considered a reasonable markup for his merchandise (I think, unbelievably, it was only 15% on most items), and, once he had marked an item, he would not vary the price unless it was damaged.

The Jewish merchants did business in an entirely different way. Their asking price was much higher (sometimes, items were marked up as much as 100%), but they were willing to negotiate the actual sales price. (My dad called that negotiation "jewing down" the price.) My dad resented that business practice. While he was friendly with the neighboring merchants, none of them were real friends. Of course, I know now what I did not know then—that the Jewish merchants were transacting business the way most merchants in the world have done for centuries.

As a teenager four of my good friends were Jewish—two boys and two girls. Lewis Millender, two years younger, and I were close friends. We worked on merit badges collaboratively, hiked and camped together, and participated in some of the same school activities, the newspaper in particular. We even traveled cross country to the National Scout Jamboree in California, sharing an upper bunk on the train. I don't remember my parents ever questioning my friendship with Lewis. (He joined me at Emory two years after I arrived there, and our friendship continued throughout my college years.)

The two Jewish girls I was friendly with attended my Methodist youth group regularly. One of them, Raina Stein, three years younger, became my first real girlfriend. (I was madly in love with Nancy Evans in fourth grade, but was socially retarded after that, slow to begin dating.) Soon after Raina and I started going out together, my parents voiced their objection to my dating her, simply because she was Jewish. Since, of course, I refused to discontinue our relationship, my dad denied me the use of the family car to date her. We dated anyway, thanks to friends who agreed to double date with us and provide transportation. That relationship continued through my senior year in high school. It might have ended earlier had my parents not drawn the "line in the sand."

I was stunned by my parents' response to my dating Raina. They had always trusted my judgment, seldom denying me anything. Their behavior was incomprehensible to me at the time. As I have told my story above, though, I have a clearer understanding of their conduct, without excusing their racist attitudes and actions.

I imagine that the Country Club in my hometown excluded Jews. Since my family did not have membership, I am not certain about that. There were probably other discriminatory practices, as well, that escaped my attention as a self-absorbed adolescent.

Anchel Samuels, an Orthodox Jew, was one of my closest friends during my college and law school days. We were both transfers to the Emory Atlanta campus as sophomores and both political science majors. We roomed together during my law school days prior to my marriage. We continue to be close friends.

I realize now that, although I often took friends home from college with me for a weekend, I never took Anchel. I know it must have been because I was unsure about how he would be received by my parents.

Our son Mark had a long-term relationship with a Jewish girlfriend during college and afterwards. A lovely person we grew to love, she visited on several occasions with Rose and me and with our extended family, including the golden anniversary celebration of my parents. I trust that she felt fully accepted.

My Civil War Education

Perhaps here I should discuss the Civil War, since it was not yet over in Northwest Georgia, even though General Robert E. Lee had surrendered the Confederate army at Appomattox seventy years before I was born. As mentioned earlier, Dalton was located on the main rail line between Atlanta and Chattanooga. Confederate troops had wintered there in 1863, prior to the Union Army's march to the sea, with the Battle of Atlanta as the centerpiece of that campaign.

The Dalton area had been the location of several significant battles during the War, and many families (mine included) had ancestors who had experienced the War firsthand. West Hill Cemetery, the city burial ground, included a large Confederate cemetery, and there was another ten or twelve miles south just off Highway 41. The Chickamauga Battlefield National Park was twenty miles or so north.

As an elementary school child, I remember parading each April to the Confederate Cemetery to decorate the graves of the fallen soldiers. Confederate Memorial Day (still a legal holiday in five Southern states) was probably the most important patriotic holiday in my community. (Of course, we did not observe the national holiday, which we called "Yankee" Memorial Day.)

The War and Reconstruction were still bitter memories in Dalton. Lest we forget, the authorized Southern version of the Civil War (my teacher instructed us to call it the War Between the States) was taught in all my history classes. That version insisted that the War was not about slavery but about states' rights. The South fought to preserve its "way of life," I learned. Permeating the society of my youth was an aura of reverence for the "lost cause." Animosity toward the North was still so strong that intermarriage between a Southerner and a Yankee was disapproved of. (Intermarriage between races, of course, was illegal.)

I'm sad to say that I don't remember questioning that version of the War. Nor do I remember hearing anyone else do so. *Gone with the Wind*, the Margaret Mitchell novel and the movie based on it, formed the picture in my mind.

The Church in the Center

The First Methodist Church was another central part of my formation. Every Sunday morning I was at Sunday school and morning worship. Every Sunday night I was at youth fellowship and evening worship. I was not a reluctant attendee, dragged there by my parents. (My dad attended infrequently; my mother, most Sunday mornings.) I loved being a part of the church community. It was there I learned about unconditional love and was encouraged and empowered to be a loving person, both in word and deed.

As a youth, I was an overachiever. Since I was usually the smallest kid in my class and not athletic, my focus was academics and extra-curricular activities. I was always at or very near the top of my class in grade point average. I usually became president or secretary or treasurer of whatever group I joined. During my senior year in high school, I was president of two service clubs and editor of both the newspaper and the yearbook.

I have always asked questions, a lot of questions. (My teachers either loved or hated me.) Reflecting now on the person I was at age 17, I wonder why I never asked questions about race. I have begun to suspect it was because I sensed that such questions would disrupt the life I had always known and might threaten acceptance by the nurturing community that sustained me.

Although I have no memories of being taught directly about racial separation, it was the lesson I learned every day from the society around me. The physical layout of our town declared separation. The leadership of our community presumed white supremacy. The activities of our everyday lives reflected the expectation of everyone in their "place." It was unnecessary to teach the young about "our Southern way of life." It was the only life we had ever known. It seemed as natural as the air we breathed and as necessary to our wellbeing as the food we ate.

Waking Up

In the summer between high school and college (1953), something happened that would change my life forever. For at least two previous summers I had attended a Methodist assembly for senior high students at Camp Glisson, a rustic retreat center in the northeast Georgia mountains for the churches of the North Georgia Conference. Always a "mountaintop" experience, this year's week was no exception. I can only describe it now as a "spiritual" encounter that convinced me to commit my life in service to God. I did not fully know what that meant then (I still don't) or what shape that would take, but the commitment was clear, unwavering, and persists to this day.

That life-directing experience culminated, at the end of the week, in my election to the Council of the Conference Youth Fellowship, the leadership group for youth ministry. Most of the Council members were already college students--very bright, very committed, and very thoughtful. I was immediately plunged into deep waters. They had thought about questions I had never considered, especially race. For the next three years, this group (not always the same people, since members were elected annually) would be the center of my life and would serve as the arena where my fundamental ideas about race would be shaped.

A Special Addendum: Another momentous thing occurred at Camp Glisson that summer that would alter my life forever. I met my soulmate and life-long partner, Rose Shearouse. More about that later.

Part II   The College and Law School Years

My Freshman Year

In the fall I started college at Emory University's Oxford campus, thirty-five miles southeast of Atlanta, where Emory was established in 1836.

Oxford was the "old South" in a way that was new to me. For example, an elderly black woman lived across the road and a block north from my dormitory. Her home was unpainted, really just a shack. As I recall it, she had a big, black iron wash pot in her yard, and she took in washing. That's how I and other students "did" our laundry. There seemed to be a lot of blacks around, all doing menial labor. Of course, there were no black students, and certainly no non-white faculty or staff.

My classes, perhaps for the first time in my life, were challenging. My world became larger, and I began to learn about critical thinking. I especially remember arguing with a young English professor who was trying to convince me that "you can't go home again." (Yes, we were reading Thomas Wolfe's novel.) He was right, of course, but I had not been away from home long enough to realize the truth of his assertion. But even at a first-rate liberal arts college in the South, in 1953 no one dared to discuss race.

Then, on May 17, 1954, just before my freshman year came to a close, the U.S. Supreme Court issued its unanimous decision in Brown v. Board of Education, declaring state laws establishing racial segregation in public schools to be unconstitutional. Suddenly, the subject that nobody talked about as I was growing up became the subject that everybody began to talk about. Finally, I had to decide where I would stand on the issue of race that had become and continues to be the central moral issue of our Republic.

Shortly after that watershed event, school was out, and I headed off to Camp Glisson for the summer as a counselor for junior highs and an organizer and leader of programs for middle and senior highs. Camp Glisson was still whites only and would remain so until the Methodist Church found the courage to end its segregated structure in 1970. When I returned to college in the fall, this time to the Atlanta campus, Emory University was still whites only and would remain so until 1964.

The North Georgia Conference Methodist Youth Fellowship

For the next two years (1954-56), my life was centered in the North Georgia Conference Methodist Youth Fellowship. I was re-elected to the Council during the summer, this time to serve as Treasurer, a position with considerable responsibility--for a special mission fund raised by the youth of the Conference and for handling registration for summer camps. (As I recall, we had ten weeks of camp with 250 campers each week.) The Council also planned and carried out other ambitious programs for the youth of the churches of the Conference throughout the school term.

The Council was a group of remarkable "older youth" (as we then designated those 18-23) and a few others still in high school. They were from all parts of North Georgia, and most were attending various Georgia colleges. Unlike many older church members and perhaps most of our peers, we were all "integrationists." Our creed was as simple as this: "God is our father. We are all God's children, whatever our color, and equally loved. We are created as one family. So why should we be separated?" We were all white, of course, since our churches were all white, but we shared a longing to be with our brothers and sisters of other races.

Our Conference had its offices in Wesley Memorial Methodist Church in downtown Atlanta. The Church was located on the "white" end of Auburn Avenue (yes, "sweet Auburn"). On the "other" end, beginning only a couple of blocks east, were several major black-owned businesses as well as Ebenezer Baptist Church (where Martin Luther King, Sr. was pastor).

Bill Cole, a recent graduate of Emory's seminary, not much older than the rest of us on the Council, was our Conference Youth Director, with offices in Wesley Memorial. (Bill would be my mentor and friend from then until this very day.) At least two or three days a week, I would take the bus from Emory or (after my parents gave me a car in the spring of 1955) drive to Bill's office to do Council work.

I lived on the Emory campus, took a full load of Emory classes, but was not much involved in campus life. My life during my college years was the North Georgia Methodist Youth Fellowship. (My college roommate and best friend, Fred Henderson, a good Baptist from Albany, Georgia, used to tell my classmates I was off "Nogamyf-ing." It wasn't his creation. The newspaper we published quarterly was named *Nogamyf*, an acronym for North Georgia Methodist Youth Fellowship.)

In the summer of 1955, I was again at Camp Glisson as counselor and registrar (no salary, just room and board). That was a HUGE summer in my life. I was elected President of the Conference Council, attended the Southeastern Jurisdiction Methodist Youth Conference at Lake Junaluska, North Carolina, attended the National Conference of Methodist Youth at Purdue University in West Lafayette, Indiana, and attended the National Convocation of Methodist Youth, also held at Purdue. Each one of these events significantly impacted my life and deepened my understanding of racism.

A Lake Junaluska Experience

The Youth Conference at Lake Junaluska came first. It was the first integrated conference I had ever attended. Since all its attendees were from the Southeast, most had known only segregation. The Lake Junaluska Trustees, although reluctantly permitting the integrated conference to be held there, had decreed that black attendees could not swim in the pool. We found that decree unconscionable, so we made the decision that no one would use the pool. I don't recall any opposition to the decision although, in retrospect, there must have been disagreement by some, even if silent. In a single week, I had experienced my first integrated gathering and my first protest. Things were finally changing.

National Gatherings at Purdue University

In August, I headed to Indiana on my own to participate in the National Conference of Methodist Youth. Meeting annually, this group of about 100 was comprised of the Presidents of each annual conference in the Church. Included were several black conference presidents.

This was a much more intimate gathering than the Lake Junaluska conference, with much more interaction among the participants. For the first time, I experienced blacks who seemed to be just like me. Some shared my views; some did not. They were not just a category but real human beings. Imagine that! I remember meeting Barbara Thompson, President of the black conference in the Washington, D.C. area. She was bright, articulate, and had some really good ideas. (She and my wife Rose later became "co-conspirators" in the struggle for women's rights in the church.)

The National Convocation of Methodist Youth convened immediately after the National Conference. Several thousand were in attendance including almost 100 from North Georgia. We gathered daily in a huge auditorium on the Purdue campus. A wide stage stretched across the front of the room with a floor-to-ceiling backdrop filled with questions. "Who am I? Where am I going?" The theme, as I recall, was "Living the Questions."

For most of us from Georgia it was a memorable experience. Blacks were fully integrated into the gathering; there was ample opportunity for interracial interaction; and we were introduced to some outstanding black leaders. I especially remember Bishop James Thomas from Iowa. He was not the stereotypical "black preacher," but spoke with quiet eloquence, genuineness, and personal authority.

As I rode the train home with my friends from Georgia, I tried to process what had just happened to me—three consecutive interracial encounters that had changed my life. Several of us talked about how transformative the experience had been for us. Several of us on the Conference Council became convinced that we must do something to make it possible for all those other Methodist youth back home to have a similar experience.

Another Addendum: Remember Rose Shearouse I mentioned before, the one I met at Camp Glisson two years earlier. Well, we had been together on the Conference Council during the past year and on the Camp Glisson staff all summer. Since she lived near Emory, we often worked together on Council projects and had become very good friends (just friends). She, too, had been at the Convocation and was on that "slow train to Georgia." We sat together on the train for most of the trip and talked endlessly about the future. By the time we arrived in Atlanta, it felt to me like something was happening between us, but I had no idea what to do about it. More about this later.

Back at Emory, I plunged into my junior year, doing what I had to do to maintain my academic standing. I had completed all my required courses and had decided to major in political science, expecting to go to law school after graduation. My heart and soul (and much of my time), though, was poured into the work of the Council.

I and others on the Council were determined to provide positive interracial experiences for other Methodist youth. However, how can you even talk about the subject of race when the world around you is screaming defiance, the politicians are calling for interposition, and the church leaders are too timid to speak out?

The Georgia United Christian Youth Movement

Sometimes there is a back door, though. Another office in the Wesley Memorial Church downtown was occupied by the Georgia Council of Churches, affiliated with the National Council of Churches (known to be a liberal organization) and staffed by United Church of Christ minister Ed Driscoll. The Methodist Church was a member of both the National and Georgia Councils. The Georgia Council included representatives of the Georgia Conference (the separate Methodist body in our state for blacks) in addition to representatives of my North Georgia Conference and the South Georgia Conference (both all white). Several black denominations were members as well—the African Methodist Episcopal (AME) Church, the African Methodist Episcopal Zion Church, and the Christian (perhaps still called Colored at that time) Methodist Episcopal (CME) Church. And, most importantly, the National Council had a youth organization called the United Christian Youth Movement (UCYM). Other state councils also had such groups.

Aha! We realized that, perhaps, this could be another way to reach our goal of interracial involvement. So our Conference Council, sometime early in 1956, petitioned the Georgia Council of Churches to sponsor a Georgia chapter of the United Christian Youth Movement. Overtly, this was simply an effort to provide a vehicle for ecumenical cooperation. But, covertly, it was an effort to provide a vehicle for interracial experience.

The Council finally adopted our proposal in the fall of 1956. My term as Conference Council President had ended in the summer, but, since this was my "baby," I continued to spearhead the work of organizing the chapter and was elected its first President. Assigned to be our adult advisers were two young ministers, both blacks. One was Clyde Williams, pastor of a CME Church in the Atlanta area. (He later became staff executive for the Consultation on Church Union, and even later, the President of Miles College, an historically Black college in Birmingham, Alabama.) The other was Andrew Young, the pastor of a Congregational Christian Church in Thomasville, Georgia. (Yes, that Andrew Young. He left before our first year was over to take a national staff position with UCYM at the New York office.)

We gathered quarterly, a few older youth from each of the Georgia Council's denominational groups, black and white together at last. We held our meetings in Wesley Memorial Church, one of the few places in Atlanta willing to host interracial gatherings in 1956. (There was even a Georgia law prohibiting interracial meetings in those days, although I am unaware of any state actions to enforce it.)

I don't remember much about the content of our gatherings. I don't even think we talked directly about race. But just being together, getting to know one another in spite of our racial differences, was transformative for many of us (especially me). And, to be completely honest, the excitement of doing that which had been forbidden, acting out our ideals, speaking our truth, living out our convictions, and, yes, defying our elders was also propelling us.

Finding My Soulmate

Something else was happening in my life in 1956. Rose Shearouse and I had become <u>very</u> close friends. Following that long train ride together the year before and our soul-searching conversations, she had returned home and declared that she was a pacifist and could not go to North Georgia College, a state military college. Both her sisters and their husbands were graduates of NGC, and she was already enrolled to begin her freshman year there in the fall. Further, she said that she wanted to go to Emory. Her father was the Assistant State School Superintendent with numerous "contacts," so he managed to get her enrolled at Emory for the fall term beginning in less than a month. Consequently, we became college mates in addition to good friends and co-workers on the Conference Council (still just good friends).

One Saturday in late spring, though, after spending the day together doing a Conference Council project with several others, Rose and I decided to go to a drive-in movie, just the two of us. We had done many things together over the past two years, after all we were close friends, but we had never done anything that remotely resembled a "date." I have no idea what film was showing that night. Neither of us really cared. In the semi-darkness of that intimate setting, I was able to tell her that I loved her, and she was able to reciprocate. From that moment on, I never doubted that she was the one with whom I wanted to spend my life. She and I were already soul friends, sharing one another's values and commitments. After another summer together working at Camp Glisson, our lives were inseparably woven together—"like peas and carrots," to quote Forrest Gump.

An Experience at Brevard and Oxford

Even in the glow of new-found love, my education about racism continued. That summer I had been named to a four-year term as a "youth" member of the Church's General Board of Social and Economic Relations, representing the Southeastern Jurisdiction. That experience would enable me to see racism through lenses clearer than my provincial eyesight had heretofore allowed. Much more about this later.

As a General Board "youth" member, I was again included with Conference Presidents in the annual meeting of the National Conference of Methodist Youth, meeting that year at Brevard College in North Carolina. Again, the Conference was an exhilarating interracial experience. My "lesson," though, came after the Conference was over.

I had ridden to North Carolina with my friend Virgil Eady III, the new North Georgia Conference President. When he learned that two attendees needed a ride to Atlanta, he offered to transport them. One was President of the South Georgia Conference, a white college student, and the other was President of the black Louisiana Conference. Both were female. In 1956 one did not travel interracially in the South without risk. I don't recall anything about the trip, so it must have been without incident. However, when it began to get dark, Virgil realized we were not going to make connections in Atlanta, so he said, "No problem. You can all stay at my house, and we'll go on to Atlanta tomorrow."

His house was actually the President's Home at the Oxford Campus of Emory University, where his father was Dean. You will recall my earlier description of Oxford as "the old South." The President's Home was a rambling antebellum structure, with lots of bedrooms. Steeped in early Methodist history, it had once, I believe, been the home of Bishop James Osgood Andrew. Bishop Andrew, a slave owner, had been suspended from exercising his office by the Methodist Episcopal Church in 1844 until he gave up his slaves. The ensuing dispute resulted in a split between the northern and southern churches, a division that did not end until 1939.

When we arrived, Virgil's mother met us at the door. She was effusive in her welcome, and, when Virgil announced that we had come to spend the night, she, as the saying goes, "never batted an eye." I doubt that a person of color, other than a servant, had ever spent a night there. I knew that, if the watchful eyes of the surrounding residents had observed our arrival, there might very well have been repercussions. We left the next morning, and I never discussed the incident with Virgil.

What I learned, though, from that experience and the example of the Eady family, is that I should never allow the specter of what others might think or do interfere with my doing what I know to be right.

General Board of Social and Economic Relations

The General Board of Social and Economic Relations was the social justice arm of the Church. Racial justice was high on its agenda, and the four years I was a member, 1956-60, were crucial years in its life. Meetings were held twice a year, and its membership was widely diverse—lay and clergy (including bishops), male and female, American and people from other countries, young and old, progressive and conservative. For almost all its members (but not all), the continuing reality of segregated structures and racial discrimination within the denomination were not only an embarrassment but an abomination. For the first time in my life, I was surrounded by a host of like-minded Christians, committed not only to a vision of equality and justice but determined to make that vision a reality. It was exhilarating!

There were numerous times during those four years that I was challenged in my thinking, my relationships, and my commitments. As I grew into full adulthood, I was encouraged to grow into full humanity. I was surrounded by a host of role models for living in beloved community while challenging those who would exclude and discriminate. Two events float to the top of the pool of my memories from those days.

I remember a plea for help the Board received from a young minister serving a small church in west Georgia. Racist tracts were being distributed by churches throughout his community, and he needed something similar to counter them. They promoted a "biblical" view of the story of Noah in which God condemns "colored" people, identified with Noah's son Ham, to perpetual inferiority and servitude. That minister was James Wall, who later became Editor of Christian Century.

Most Board members were far removed from rural life in the South and could hardly imagine the context of Wall's plea. Even though a Southerner with rural roots, I too lacked understanding of the depths of racism and the sacrifice required from those on the frontlines of the struggle for racial justice.

The Board responded by providing alternative resources, which may or may not have been helpful. One positive outcome did occur; my comprehension of the level of commitment required to resist racism was deepened.

One of the Board's most vocal members was John Satterfield, a white attorney from Hattiesburg, Mississippi. John seemed to understand his role to be the defense of the South and its "way of life." He assumed that, since I too was from the South, I should be his ally. He quickly learned that I had less tolerance for his racist views than other, more charitable Board members.

Although permitted to make his argument as each issue was debated, John felt that his perspective was not being fully understood. Wanting to be abundantly fair, the Board leadership acceded to John's request to make a formal speech at one of our luncheons explaining his views. I remember being seated at a table with the black Bishop from New Orleans, Willis King, on my right. Claire Harvey, an articulate black woman from the same town as John, sat on my left.

Sitting through John's defense of white supremacy and his "scientific" explanation of racial inferiority was one of the most painful experiences of my life. I could only imagine what Bishop King and Ms. Harvey were thinking and feeling. I wish someone (me?) had stood up and demanded that he cease the violence he was committing against us all, but especially the blacks in our company. However, we all politely sat, looking down, squirming in our seats, taking it.

I learned that free speech isn't free; it's costly to those who receive the blows of that speech. I learned that sitting quietly, permitting the obscenity of racist speech, is enabling that behavior. I learned that politeness is less important than protecting our fellow human beings from verbal abuse.

Beginning my senior year, academics assumed a higher priority. I had decided to go to law school, and grades became more important. Getting married became even more important to us as well. To expedite that union, we gave up summer breaks and sacrificed many of the activities that had claimed our devotion in the past. Rose completed her English degree and earned a certificate to teach secondary education in December 1958. I finished my political science degree in June 1957 and my law degree in August 1959. Because of the generosity of our parents, who continued to finance our schooling, we were able to be married in August 1958.

While we were focusing on our education, we were keenly aware of the stranglehold segregation still had on the South, but we could see as well that the struggle for racial justice was beginning to gain momentum. During my senior year I continued my work with the Georgia United Christian Youth Movement, experiencing the gift of friendship beyond racial difference. I also continued to attend the twice-yearly meetings of the General Board of Social and Economic Relations, experiencing the inspiration of leaders working for racial change in the church.

The Central Jurisdiction

While I was in my first year of law school, a special Commission of the Methodist Church announced hearings all over the country to hear from the grassroots about how to deal with its segregated structure.

.
The Methodist Church had been created by a reunion. The original Methodist denomination, formed in 1784, had split in 1844 in a dispute over slavery. The Methodist Episcopal Church (mostly Northern) and the separate Methodist Episcopal Church South were the result of that division. In order to reunite them in 1939, the "new" church was divided into five jurisdictions based on geography and one jurisdiction based on race. In Georgia, the white churches were divided into two Conferences--North Georgia and South Georgia. They were a part of the Southeastern Jurisdiction. The black churches were in a separate conference--the Georgia Conference. That conference was part of a separate jurisdiction--the Central Jurisdiction. That jurisdiction included all the black churches in the country.

When I learned that one of the hearings would be held in downtown Atlanta at Wesley Memorial Church, I knew I wanted to speak. After all, I had been President of the North Georgia Conference youth organization and was a member of a general board whose agenda included race relations. I believed that the voices of youth should especially be heard since we would be living most of our lifetime with the consequences of this decision. (I acknowledge a bit of arrogance, as well.)

What I had to say seemed indisputable to me, based on that simple creed I mentioned earlier: "God is our father. We are all God's children, whatever our color, and equally loved. We are created as one family. So why should we be separated?" My "solution" was also simple—abolish the Central Jurisdiction and add the African American churches to the five jurisdictions based on geography.

Rose went with me to the hearing, of course, and we took our seats beside two older women from North Georgia whom we knew and respected, knowing they would be supportive. They were Mattie Trimble, widow of the dean of the seminary at Emory and former president of the North Georgia Conference women's organization, who would be one of those speaking for abolishing the separate jurisdiction for blacks. The other was Mrs. M. E. Tilly (Dorothy Rogers Tilly, but she always insisted on being called by her husband's name). Mrs. Tilly had been on President Truman's Civil Rights Commission and was, at the time, Director of the Southern Regional Council, an Atlanta civil rights organization. These two women are my all-time favorite activists.

The hearing panel was chaired by a black pastor from Los Angeles, Charles Golden (later elected a bishop). There must have been ten or twelve members of the panel from across the country. I don't remember whether or not there were other blacks on the panel. (I just realized as I was writing this that no blacks were in the audience. Since these were called jurisdictional hearings, ours must have been exclusively for the Southeastern Jurisdiction, which included white churches only. A separate hearing was probably held for the Central Jurisdiction churches.)

As soon as the hearing was opened, Bishop Arthur J. Moore from Atlanta, who was also President of the Jurisdictional College of Bishops, was recognized to speak. His position was as simple as mine. The basis of the 1939 reunion agreement, he argued, was the separate Central Jurisdiction for black churches. He insisted that, without that separation, there would be another split in the church. Speaking for all the Southeastern bishops, he turned to the audience, addressing primarily the many ministers in attendance, and threatened retaliation if anyone dared take a contrary position. Consequently, only one minister did, George Foster from Florida. In addition to Dr. Foster, Mrs. Trimble, and me, there were only two others advocating change—an attorney from Ft. Lauderdale and a church social worker from Augusta.

Following the hearing, the pastor of my home church in Dalton, Delma Hagood, confronted me in the hallway. "How dare you?" he shouted in my face, threatening me with exposure to racist relatives at home. That proved to be an empty threat since the next morning's edition of the *Atlanta Constitution* printed an account of the hearing on its front page, naming me and quoting a part of my remarks.

My mother reported that my father had been upset about the incident, although he never spoke to me about it. He was probably more concerned about the embarrassment resulting from the publicity than about my actions. My parents had always supported me, respecting my judgment, never attempting to control my behavior, and they continued to do so this time as well. More importantly, they continued to fund my education.

Of course, in spite of the overwhelming opposition to change in the Southeast, the Commission recommended abolition of the Central Jurisdiction, and the whole Church, even the Southeast, slowly began to implement that change. More about that later.

What did I learn from this incident? I learned that doing what is right will not always be valued, especially by people with institutional power whose self-interest is tied to maintaining the status quo. I learned to trust my inner voice, even though others with more experience and more authority might oppose me. I discovered within myself the courage to stand up for my convictions in spite of potential negative consequences.

Part III The Law Years

In the Middle District of Georgia

On a hot summer day in July of 1959, I was sitting in the library of the law school studying for my final, final exams. I was startled when the Administrative Assistant to the Dean tapped me on the shoulder, summoning me to the Dean's Office. When I arrived there, I learned that the Dean had just received a call from U.S. District Judge William Augustus Bootle requesting that I call him.

I had taken and passed the Georgia bar exam in February and had been "sworn in" and licensed to practice in June. In fact, I had already been working part-time that summer as an attorney for Atlanta Legal Aid, but I had made no effort to find a permanent job. The reason? I had deferred my compulsory military service during my six years of higher education and expected to be drafted as soon as I graduated.

Of course, I immediately called Judge Bootle and was astonished to learn that he wanted me to come to Macon to be interviewed for a position as his law clerk. I expressed my keen interest in the job but explained my military draft situation. I had been hoping to fulfill my obligation through six months of active duty and the remainder in the reserves, but there was no guarantee that option would be available, I noted. No problem, he said. If he decided to hire me, I could take a leave of absence and return when my service was complete. He asked that Rose accompany me to the interview (probably the reason I was hired). Thus began a 20-month chapter of my life that would introduce me to the "deep South" and open my eyes about government-imposed racism. (When I went for my draft physical in the fall, I was rejected; I weighed less than the required minimum for inductees. It was perhaps the only time in my life I rejoiced that I was "skinny.")

The Middle District of Georgia stretches diagonally from the Northeast to the Southwest. Court is held in each of seven locations—Athens, Macon (its headquarters), Americus, Albany, Columbus, Valdosta, and Thomasville. The Court staff includes Clerks, District Attorneys, Probation Officers, Marshalls, and the Judge's Staff of a Secretary, Law Clerk, and Court Reporter. They travel to each location twice a year to hold court for as long as necessary to accommodate the current docket. Consequently, close relationships are developed; the Court staff becomes like family (at least that was my experience).

Judge Bootle grew up in Round O, a tiny town in South Carolina plantation country. He was schooled in the "Southern way of life" from birth, and he had accepted that "way" without questioning it. He was appointed Judge for the Middle District by President Eisenhower (only three days after the Supreme Court's decision in Brown v. Board of Education). He became a brilliant jurist, partly because he "loved the law," as I often heard him say. He was never an "integrationist," although his rulings paved the way for an integrated society in the State. He was a man of unimpeachable integrity, setting aside his personal feelings and following the law and its precedents without regard to personal consequences.

My job was, primarily, to write opinions. I was 24; Judge Bootle was 57. I was just out of law school; he was an experienced trial lawyer and district attorney, a former law school professor and dean, and a seasoned judge. Yet he treated me as his equal. After hearing arguments and reading briefs, he might reach a tentative decision, but he usually wanted me to question it if I had a contrary opinion. I could sometimes change his mind. Sometimes, he wanted to know what I thought even before he began to ponder his decision. It was an intellectually exhilarating experience.

Three "equal protection of the law" cases, all decided in 1960 during my tenure as law clerk, stand out in my memory. I was the primary writer of the opinion in each of those cases, and racism was central to the conduct under scrutiny. Two of them were historically significant.

Integration of the University of Georgia

The first, Holmes v. Danner, challenged the practice of denying blacks admission to the University of Georgia. At the time of the lawsuit, more than five years after Brown v. Board of Education, no school at any level in the State of Georgia was integrated. The State legislature had even enacted a statute withholding funds from any school that dropped its color barrier.

The plaintiffs, Hamilton Holmes (who would later become a member of the Emory University medical faculty) and Charlayne Hunter (who became the renowned journalist

Charlayne Hunter-Gault on PBS) were outstanding graduates of Atlanta high schools. They had been carefully selected by the NAACP Legal Defense Fund for this test case. Donald Hollowell, a prominent black attorney in Atlanta, and Constance Baker Motley, an NAACP staff attorney (later a U.S. Circuit Court judge), argued their case.

B. D. Murphy, another prominent Atlanta lawyer, and State Attorney General Eugene Cook were the attorneys of record for the University. (Coincidentally, Attorney General Cook was the uncle of my wife Rose's brother-in-law.) They presented a convoluted plethora of evidence attempting to establish that Mr. Holmes and Ms. Hunter had been denied admission for perfectly legitimate reasons that had nothing to do with their race.

The trial in Athens was a farce. Mr. Danner, the University Registrar, and his associates squirmed in the witness chair as Ms. Motley conducted a brilliant and searing cross-examination. Everyone present in the courtroom, especially the defendants, knew the real reason for the denial of admission, but we all had to pretend that we were witnessing a serious trial of facts.

At the conclusion of the trial, after Judge Bootle had issued his order directing admission, the political fireworks began. When appeals had been exhausted and Holmes and Hunter were on campus, Governor Ernest Vandiver (married to Betty Russell, niece of powerful U.S. Senator Richard B. Russell) ordered Georgia National Guard troops to Athens to "protect" them from protests that had erupted on campus. They were removed from their campus residences "for their safety." However, they soon returned to the Athens campus after Judge Bootle enjoined further interference by the Governor. Both students stayed to complete their degrees.

Three memories stand out about that trial. The first is watching Judge Bootle struggle over how he would address the plaintiffs and their attorneys. I know that sounds trivial, but it was not. Throughout the South, courtesy titles (Mr., Miss, Mrs.) were not customarily used in addressing blacks, even in courtrooms. To do so would violate the unwritten cultural code. As was often the case, Judge (as I addressed him) discussed his dilemma with me. (One of my roles was to be his sounding board.) I suggested he think about how it would look in the court record on appeal if he had failed to use courtesy titles. I don't know the impact of my question, but I do know that he chose to use courtesy titles, preferring, however, to address the black lawyers as "Counselor" or "Attorney" whenever possible.

My second vivid memory is watching Ms. Motley, lead attorney for the plaintiffs, in action in the courtroom. As I recall, she was a statuesque woman, ebony in color. She always wore black and was a commanding presence. As she questioned witnesses, Mr. Murphy, lead attorney for the University, constantly interrupted with objections, many of them frivolous, seeking to rattle her and suggest desired responses to his witnesses. Once the judge had ruled on the objection, she would, unhurriedly and in a firm and authoritative voice, ask the court reporter to repeat the question. In my sheltered world, I had never seen such a performance. I wanted to be just like her.

My third memory is watching Registrar Danner struggle to defend the elaborate scheme the University had concocted to deny access to the plaintiffs. I especially recall a letter Ms.

Motley forced him to read on the stand. The letter tried to explain to a prominent alumnus why his "legacy" daughter could not be admitted at that time because, to do so, might jeopardize the University's claim of non-discrimination. I suspected that Mr. Danner was not in agreement with the University's position but, like so many other Southerners at the time, lacked the courage to stand up against the politicians in power and the people who supported them.

Voting Rights in Terrell County

The second case, United States v. Raines, was the first action brought by the Department of Justice under the Civil Rights Act of 1957. It sought to prevent the Voting Registrars of Terrell County from depriving certain named persons of voting rights on account of their race or color. In the initial decision, Chief Judge Hoyt Davis had ruled the Act unconstitutional in 1959 (before my tenure with the Court). On appeal the U.S. Supreme Court had reversed that decision, and it had been remanded for trial before Judge Bootle. That trial was held without a jury in Americus in 1960.

Terrell County (county seat, Dawson) is located between Albany and Americus. It is majority black, but, in 1958, there were only 48 Negro (the term then used) citizens registered to vote out of 2,858 total voters. The State had passed a new law in 1958 to help curb black voter registration. It required that applicants demonstrate before the Board of Registrars literacy in reading and writing the Constitution or answer correctly 20 out of 30 questions on a written citizenship test.

The trial revealed that Terrell County had systematically denied the vote to Negro citizens by identifying their applications using different colors and by keeping separate records; by delaying action; and by administering literacy tests differently while requiring higher standards for Negro applicants. (Applicants "failing" the test included two with master's degrees and five with bachelor's degrees. Six were teachers in the county school system and one was county agent.)

The Court ordered the immediate registration of several of the applicants and enjoined future discrimination by the Registrars.

Although I had already been aware of discrimination in voting in Georgia, I was nevertheless amazed at the machinations that were being employed to maintain white control. These upright citizens, pillars of their local churches, apparently had no qualms about their actions. They were clearly not seeing blacks as equal citizens and full human beings.

I was particularly intrigued by Jimmy Raines, Chair of the Board of Registrars. He was a young man (still in his 30s) and clearly at the apex of the local establishment. He was a Harvard Law School graduate and had been a Rhodes Scholar. As I watched his testimony I wondered how, in spite of that exposure, he could continue to engage in such blatant unjust practices. (Testimony revealed, for example, that he had dictated a portion of the Constitution so rapidly that the applicant could not possibly write it and then declared his work illegible.)

A peculiar thing happened on the day of the next election following this decision. The Judge received a call from the mother of Jimmy Raines. She was at her polling place in Dawson, and she believed the election officials were violating the Judge's order in how they were conducting the voting. The

Judge talked with her, but explained that he could not become involved except through the attorneys. When a hearing in the case was held later the next year, I noted that Jimmy Raines was no longer Chair of the Board of Registrars.

Koinonia Farm and the Americus School Board

The third case, Wittkamper v. Harvey, did not have the historical significance of the other two, and it involved a much simpler set of facts, largely undisputed. Will Wittkamper and two other high school students were Sumter County residents living outside the bounds of the City of Americus. James Harvey and the other members of the Americus Board of Education had promulgated a policy permitting students living in the county to attend city schools upon request. Wittkamper and his fellow Koinonia students had made such a request but had been denied admission. All other county students applying had been admitted.

The Board conceded that its decision was based on their residence at Koinonia Farm, a communal Christian community. The Board argued that it had the right to deny admission for any reason. However, it insisted that its decision in this instance had been made to avoid "trouble and disorder that would immediately result from their acceptance."

The highlight of the trial came with the testimony of Clarence Jordan, Koinonia's founder. Dr. Jordan was a minister ordained by the Southern Baptist Convention and had earned a Ph.D. in New Testament Greek from Southern Baptist Theological Seminary in Louisville. (Incidentally, he was also part of a prominent political family in Georgia, the uncle of Hamilton Jordan, later chief of staff to President Jimmy Carter.)

With a handful of other families, Clarence and his wife Florence had established Koinonia Farm as a place for several families to live out the teachings of Jesus together. The families, although living separately, held all possessions in common following the model of the early Christian community. They were pacifists, rejecting all violence. They practiced acceptance of all human beings, regardless of race, as brothers and sisters. Although no black family was resident at the Farm at the time, they had been an interracial community in the past and were willing to be so again.

Judge Bootle, also a devout Southern Baptist, listened intently as Dr. Jordan explained the beliefs and practices of the Koinonia community. He spoke with such clarity and genuineness that the entire courtroom seemed to hang on to every word he uttered. Judge Bootle even participated in the questioning, exhibiting the curiosity and openness that were so much a part of his character.

The law in this case was clear. While the Americus Board had the right to exclude all county students from admission to its schools, if it decided to admit any county students, it must do so in a non-discriminatory manner. In excluding those who resided at Koinonia Farm, it had failed to accord them "equal protection of the laws." Therefore, the Court ordered their admission.

Addendum: Koinonia Farm, incidentally, started Koinonia Partners, a project to provide affordable housing for poor people in the area, many of them black. That project evolved to become Habitat for Humanity, the amazing worldwide effort to do the same for the whole planet.

While this decision had little impact outside Sumter County, it elicited deep-seated feelings there. In addition, remember that Judge Bootle had recently ordered the Board of Registrars in neighboring Terrell County to register black voters, and had, only months earlier, ordered the University of Georgia to admit its first black students.

What happened next was not a complete surprise. When the traveling Court family arrived in Americus on the Sunday night before its next regular session following this decision, there was an effigy of the Judge hanging on a makeshift gallows on the courthouse lawn. (Americus was the only District site without a federal courthouse. Court sessions were held instead in the County courthouse.)

Needless to say, there were some tense moments that night. We had only two or three U.S. marshals for protection, and no one believed that local law enforcement officers could be relied on to come to our aid if needed. The night was without incident, though. When Court was convened the next morning, Judge Bootle used his considerable powers of persuasion to convince all attorneys involved in the cases on the docket to either settle or continue their cases to the next term. We were out of town before dark.

Since this is the final story about my experience with the Court, I want to reflect on the remarkable but complex man who was my boss, my mentor, and my friend—Judge Bootle. Judge was certainly a man of his time and place—a "dyed in the wool" Southern gentleman, born at the beginning of the 20th century, schooled in the "ways" of the South and never, at least when I was his clerk, completely free of the shackles of white superiority and racial prejudice. However, unlike several other federal judges in the South, he was a jurist of impeccable character who was devoted to the law and determined to follow it wherever it led him, regardless of his personal feelings and in spite of personal consequences.

After he made the rulings mentioned earlier, he was bombarded with hate communications. His father, then in his 80s, refused further communication with him. Nevertheless, he persevered. He lived to be 102, still mentally alert with his insatiable curiosity continuing to drive him. He lived long enough, fortunately, to see the federal building and courthouse in Macon renamed for him.

I learned many things as Judge Bootle's law clerk--about myself, about the persistence of racism in public life, and about the administration of justice in the segregated South. Most importantly, though, I learned that the legal system of our Republic, when administered by persons of integrity even if still flawed by racist conditioning, can be a vehicle for correcting the racism that haunts us.

I have hesitated to include the following paragraph but, since this memoir is probably my last word, decided to do so anyway. A few days before I left my job with the Court, Judge Bootle's secretary, Anita Cain, who had become my close friend and confidante, asked me, "Have you ever wondered why Judge called you to come for an interview?" When I answered that, of course I'd wondered, she told me this story. When his previous law clerk decided to leave, Judge called his good friend Ed Smith, a Columbus attorney who was a member of the State Board of Bar Examiners, asking for the names of the five top scorers on the latest bar exam. Although scores on bar exams were never revealed, simply pass or fail, he gave him a list of five names. "Now, Ed," Judge said. "Which one had the highest score?" Ed pointed to my name.

Taking a Different Road

The circuit-riding life with the Court had been a joy, particularly because my wife Rose could travel with me. Early in 1961, though, she was pregnant, much to our delight, and such a life would, we realized, no longer be feasible. So I began the search for a "rest of my life" job. With a strong reference from Judge Bootle, I was able to land a position as an associate of a leading law firm in Atlanta--Gambrell, Harlan, Russell, Moye & Richardson. Smythe Gambrell, the managing partner, had been a president of the American Bar Association, and the firm largely represented big corporations, Eastern Air Lines being the major client. We bought a new house in the suburbs, moved in temporarily with Rose's parents while it was being completed, and awaited the birth of our first son, who inconveniently arrived early on June 9, weeks before the house was finished.

Then began my "dark night of the soul." (No, Mark, you did not cause it, although your birth was probably the catalyst for my reexamining where my life was headed.) You may recall that I earlier described a "spiritual" encounter in 1953 that convinced me to commit my life in service to God. I indicated that I did not fully know what that meant or what shape it would take, but my commitment was clear and unwavering.

Up until Mark's birth, I thought I could fulfill my commitment through the practice of law. I did not question that during my tenure with the Court. However, I now began to have doubts about it. I had many sleep-deprived nights that summer. Mark had colic and would sometimes cry for three hours before falling asleep. As if that were not enough, I would be unable to go back to sleep, agonizing over the direction my life had taken and asking whether I had lost my way.

One long night in July or August, while pacing the floor, trying to find a comfortable position to relieve Mark's pain, a poignant scene from Rodgers and Hammerstein's musical *Carousel* began to play in my head. Billy Bigelow, having learned that he is to become a father, soliloquizes about his role and what it means for his life. Unfortunately, his conclusion and resulting behavior are disastrous for all concerned. Nevertheless, his struggle helped me clarify mine. I knew that I wanted my life to be true to my commitment of service to God and worthy of emulation. While not yet an "answer," I had found a "direction."

The life I had commenced when I joined the Gambrell firm was wholly centered in the wellbeing of the firm and its clients. We all worked at least six days a week. (The ultimate symbol was that firm meetings were held at 7:00 a.m. on Saturday mornings.) Our social lives were expected to further the practice—which most often meant entertaining clients. I remember being told that involvement with church on Sunday was a good thing because it provided an opportunity to expand our client base. Even the way we dressed was prescribed. A fellow associate, for example, let me know that Mr. Gambrell believed that a lawyer was worth twice as much if he wore a hat. I wanted to respond by asking if he would double my salary if I did. Instead, I said nothing, and bought myself a hat. As a consequence, I began to lose my self-respect.

The work I did during my short tenure was less than inspiring. The cases that occupied my days were almost exclusively about money, and the accumulation of money had never had much meaning for me. (Rose, who knew me better than anyone else ever has, believed that "having meaning" was as necessary for me as food and water.) I was miserable! Happily married to my soulmate, in my "dream job," a proud new father, a first-time homeowner, seemingly "set" for the rest of my life, how could I possibly be unhappy? But could I face "this" for the rest of my working life? Where had I gone wrong? What could I do to "fix" it?

My intense soul-searching led me back to those experiences in which I had felt most alive, most creative, of most value, most faithful to my life commitment—my work in the Church. So the answer became clear. I would quit my job, go to seminary, and become an ordained minister. What a moment of grace it was when Rose enthusiastically supported me in that decision.

Part IV   Seminary and Ordination

The Seminary Years

Acting quickly once I've made a decision has been one of my characteristics throughout life (although tempered during the years of my marriage since Rose did not share that trait). By September, I had resigned my job with the Gambrell firm, secured admission to Candler School of Theology at Emory University with a full-tuition scholarship, arranged a part-time job in youth ministry at a large Atlanta church (Peachtree Road

Methodist), and begun the first step of the ordination process. We continued to live in our house since our neighborhood, still under construction, made our house not very marketable.

I had calculated that, barring unforeseen circumstances, our savings accumulated during my time with the Court, my scholarship, and the income from my part-time job would see us through the three years of seminary. It did, but just barely. At the end of my first year, I traded the Peachtree Road job for a position as Associate Conference Youth Director (nice sounding title, gratifying work, paltry compensation). Again, I was spending my summers directing programs at Camp Glisson while, during the regular school year, working with the Conference Council planning youth programs for the churches of the Conference.

Although my days were filled almost beyond their capacity, I thrived on my studies and the work I was doing. For Rose, though, alone in the suburbs with a baby and no car, it was, to quote her, "a bleak time." (How bleak I did not fully understand until I read her memoir written in the last year of her life.)

Seminary was an intellectually stimulating time for me—a time of discovering new "answers" to my questions about God and the meaning of life that were more adequate than the simpler beliefs of my youth, but also a time of discovering new questions, many of which, hopefully, will always engage me. Emory was still barring black students (letting the threat of loss of tax exemptions from the State determine its policy), and, of course, there were no black faculty or staff members. Certainly, though, most of the faculty members supported racial inclusiveness. I especially remember Clinton Gardner, Professor of Christian Ethics, and Earl Brewer, Professor of Sociology and Religion, as ones providing a theological foundation for my "gut" feelings about racism.

One particular seminary classroom experience related to my "education" about racism is etched in my memory. In my final year, I was taking a required course on the Discipline of the Methodist Church. The Discipline is the "law book" of the Church, and the course was being taught by Retired Bishop Costen J. Harrell. Bishop Harrell had been one of the primary authors of the Discipline adopted in 1939 when the Church was reunited. With my law background and Bishop Harrell's expertise, I thought this course would provide a wonderful learning experience.

One particular class session was focused on the Discipline's provisions related to church membership. Bishop Harrell pointed out that, unlike Baptist churches, Methodist church pastors admit members solely on the basis of confession of faith without a vote of the congregation. I immediately raised my hand to ask the following question: "If an African American comes forward seeking church membership in a previously all-white church, should not that person be accepted on the basis of confession of faith, then, just as a white person would be?" Bishop Harrell responded that the church's administrative board should first be consulted. I argued, in response, that to do so would be to violate the Discipline. It goes without saying that I did not win that argument, although I remain convinced that, except for racism, my conclusion was unassailable.

I learned that, even in the Church, there is one "law" for whites and another for blacks. I learned, once again, that the Church's leaders, too, are tainted by the racism shaping our society.

My job with the Conference Youth Ministry commanded all my surplus energy during my final two years of seminary. Although I was in a different role than I had been as an "older youth," I thrived on the close relationships and creative team work necessary for effective ministry. The year before I began, the Conference Youth Council had sponsored its very first interracial gathering. It was held at Camp Glisson, not the most liberal location in the State. (As a matter of fact, Lumpkin County, its site, adjoined Forsyth County, which boasted that the sun would never set on a "N-word" there.) Although the gathering had proceeded without incident, the Camp Manager, a deputy sheriff, reportedly was armed and ready to protect the Camp if necessary. The "older youth" leaders were rightly proud of their successful breakthrough in race relations.

Summer camp and the Conference youth program continued to be a white-only experience, though, since the Church was still segregated. The only other interracial experience available for youth at the time was the Georgia United Christian Youth Movement (see above), which continued to provide ecumenical and interracial experiences for a few.

Our summer camp and conference program often included an international student from one of the Methodist colleges as part of the leadership team for a week or two. In the summer of 1962 that student was Olivia Masih. Olivia (we called her Olive then) was from Jabalpur, India, and had just come to Dallas to study at Southern Methodist University. Her skin was dark, but she almost always wore a sari, making her acceptable as an "exotic" in many places not welcoming to dark-skinned African Americans.

On a weekend Olivia was with us, the leadership team decided to go on an outing to a local copper mine. Olivia wore "American" clothes like the others. While they were in the mine, they were accosted by some locals who objected to this "mixed" group. Feeling unsafe, they left and were followed all the way back to camp. Fortunately, nothing further occurred. Olivia became a close family friend that summer and continues so today. More about Olivia later.

While my life was focused on the camping program in the summer, conference youth programming and a full load of classes during the academic year, the civil rights movement was gaining momentum throughout the South. That momentum reached its peak in the summer of 1963 with the March on Washington in August. I was in Macon, Georgia, that week—leading a Youth Week for senior highs. The special program was being held at Mulberry Street Methodist Church downtown, where Rose and I had been senior high counselors when I worked for the Court. On the day of the March, while at the church preparing for the evening gathering, I went into a lounge where the long-time black custodian was watching the telecast of the March. As I sat with him, watching his face as we listened to those emotion-charged speeches, I had an epiphany. For blacks who had never known freedom as I experienced it routinely, the movement was life-giving to a degree I could never fully comprehend. I wanted, more than ever before, to be a part of it.

Even with seminary graduation and ordination happening at the end of spring in 1964, the most momentous event by far was the birth of our son Bryan. Like his brother, he came early, April 27, almost causing me to fail a required course that my graduation and ordination depended on. We had postponed having a second child for obvious reasons, but this desired pregnancy was timed about right—just not that particular day. We rejoiced to have our family complete as we began a new chapter in our lives.

Ordination

The Methodist Church, unlike most other Protestant denominations, requires two ordinations. (Our ordination "juice" must be weaker than others' since it takes two "doses" to create our clergy.) I was seeking to become part of the "traveling" ministry—that is, those subject to annual appointment to a place of ministry by the Bishop and his Cabinet (the district superintendents). I had been ordained a Deacon at the end of my first seminary year. My second ordination as an Elder would follow my graduation in June.

As I contemplated my second ordination, I became increasingly aware that my personal theology differed from the Church's orthodoxy; I hoped it was compatible. I had recently read John A.T. Robinson's *Honest to God*, the tradition-shattering classic published earlier that year, and began to wonder how I was going to reconcile Bishop Robinson's questions with the Church's answers. (I'm still wondering, by the way.) I had become aware, too, that the Christian life, as I was experiencing it, is not so much about belief as about action. My twenty-nine years as a Southern "white boy" had also taught me that racial justice is at the center of the action Christian faith demands. Therefore, I knew that ministry for me would always include addressing in word and deed the issue of racism. I had begun to sense, as well, how deep the roots of racism have penetrated the church, our society, and our souls.

Part V   LaGrange and Oakwood

Ma Barton and the Barton Trust

I am inserting here a piece of my story that is like a thread running through several decades. I first met and fell in love with Etta Pursley Barton (we all called her "Ma") when her husband, J. Hamby Barton, Sr., came to be my pastor in Dalton the summer before my senior year in high school. She encouraged me unreservedly and challenged me by the way she lived and loved. Soon after I finished seminary, she asked both Rose and me to be trustees of her trust, a role we fulfilled until her death in 1992. We contributed regularly to the Trust, and I managed the finances for many of those years.

Ma had created the trust (originally named Student Educational Foundation) to help her "care for" international students studying in the U.S. She had been offering a "home away from home" for these special students for years, but, when two Korean students studying at Woman's College of Georgia in Milledgeville found themselves stranded without funds during the Korean War, she created the Trust to formalize her "care." The Trust became the vehicle for providing financial support as needed, which she shamelessly solicited from everyone she knew (and some she didn't). Always thinking about the future, she groomed Rose and me to be her successor.

We immediately proposed Olivia Masih from India, studying at Southern Methodist University, to receive assistance. We had met and formed a bond with Olivia at Camp Glisson in the summer of 1963 (see above). She spent some of her Christmas break with us for two years, 1964 (in LaGrange) and 1965 (in Oakwood). Now living in Falmouth, Massachusetts (on the Cape), she remains among my treasured friends.

Several other international students will appear in my stories to follow—most notably, Neil Jen from Taiwan and Christopher Egwim from Nigeria. Although not African American, having them as a part of our family for decades has contributed to the depth of my understanding of racism in our country, particularly in the South.

(Unfortunately, members of Ma's family, who were on the Trust's Board, decided to discontinue it when she died, utilizing the funds, instead, to create a permanent scholarship at Emory's seminary. I believe she would have chosen otherwise.)

LaGrange

Having never before been in a pastoral role in a local church, following seminary I chose to be an associate pastor in a large church rather than to receive a pastoral assignment through the regular appointment system (likely two or more very small churches in a rural area). Associate pastors were generally chosen by senior pastors and merely confirmed through the appointment system. That was true in my case as well.

When Reynolds Greene, pastor of First Methodist Church in LaGrange, invited me to be his associate, I quickly accepted, primarily to avoid the alternative, even though I knew he was much more conservative than I. LaGrange was a college town, I reasoned, and the large church just off campus was surely a place I could "fit in." The college president, Waights Henry, was a casual friend. His son and I had been college classmates, and Rose had been a bridesmaid at the son's marriage to one of her college friends.

I soon learned that LaGrange shaped the college more than the college shaped LaGrange. Located near the Alabama border southwest of Atlanta and north of Columbus, LaGrange was a company town. Callaway Mills was the primary employer, and West Point Pepperell not far away ran it a close second. As was common in the culture of the time, the mill owned much of the housing and supplied other needs of its employees at an elevated cost. Benevolently, it also provided a library and a recreation center, one of each for whites and another for blacks. The white managers of the mill attended First Methodist, of course, or one of the other downtown churches.

I had known, when I accepted the offer to go to LaGrange, that race would be a hot-button issue there. The Methodist Church in Georgia was still segregated, including its local college, and public school integration was proceeding only at a snail's pace (but not at all in Troup County). Historically, this had been plantation country, and it still had a large black population descended from former slaves.

The Help

When the ladies in our church realized we had three-month-old and three-year-old sons, they insisted that we should hire part-time "help." Since I was earning the conference minimum salary, Rose explained that we could not afford such a luxury.

When one particularly insistent parishioner explained that her "help" needed additional work, we agreed to consider it. We were appalled when we learned how little she was paid. Yes, we could afford that amount, but should we employ someone for such a paltry sum? On the other hand, if she needed additional work, should we refuse to employ her because we couldn't pay more? We finally reached an uneasy compromise. We paid a higher hourly wage (still too low, but more than others were paying) but employed her for fewer hours. This moral dilemma is one that continues to haunt me to this day.

LaGrange Council on Human Relations

I knew immediately that any engagement with racial reconciliation in the community would, of necessity, be very limited if I wanted to keep my job. However, I was committed to do "something." Of course, there were other "integrationists" (or "N-word lovers," as some would prefer to call us) in the congregation, and they invited us to join the only interracial group in town, the Council on Human Relations.

The Council met monthly, on a Sunday afternoon, at either Warren Temple Methodist Church (the local black congregation) or St. Mark's Episcopal Church (all white). Although other centrally located churches had been asked to host the gatherings, only these two were willing.

Our meetings were primarily social gatherings. As I recall, we usually had fifteen or twenty blacks and a like number of whites present. Mostly, we stood around drinking punch and eating cookies, getting acquainted. But in those days and in that place, even that was controversial. A member of my congregation whom others had identified as a member of the Ku Klux Klan always sat across from our meeting location, watching who came. He never spoke to me about his surveillance. (In retrospect, I wish I had approached and invited him to join us.)

The Council was a very loose organization. I think the St. Mark's rector Bill Jones (later Episcopal Bishop of Missouri) provided primary leadership. One project I recall was undertaken at the request of the State Council. We had been asked to visit school districts in the area to ask about their plans for complying with the federal mandate to integrate schools. Rose agreed to accompany a friend from the church on a visit to the Hogansville school board office in a neighboring county to make that inquiry. Their visit had been cordial but not very informative.

That same night, I received a call from a friend in the church alerting me to potential trouble. The Hogansville superintendent, it seems, had called the LaGrange school superintendent informing him of the visit. The LaGrange superintendent had then called prominent Methodist church members to tell them what had occurred. I chose to ignore the whole incident, and don't remember anyone ever talking to me about it. (Of course, I later learned that direct confrontation is not how LaGrange dealt with controversy.)

Of even greater consequence that year was another event related to the Council. I had been asked and agreed to represent us at a state-wide conference of representatives of local Councils. When I learned that I could not attend because of church responsibilities, Rose agreed to go in my stead. Another person from our Council also attended the conference--James Brown, a leader in the local NAACP. It was being held at the Continuing

Education Center of the University of Georgia in Athens. One of the speakers scheduled on the program was James Farmer, Director of CORE (Congress of Racial Equality). The State PTA objected to his presence and mounted a campaign to force the University to deny the use of the facility. The University did not accede to the demand, and Farmer did not show after all. However, the LaGrange newspaper published an article about the controversy on its front page. On the back page, the usual notice of the monthly meeting of the LaGrange Council was printed, including the announcement that Rose and Mr. Brown would report on the Athens Conference. It was not surprising that the senior pastor, my "boss," was not pleased.

I recall one other incident involving the Council. At the Council meeting following the now famous Selma March in the spring of 1965, the Warren Temple Methodist Church pastor addressed the gathering. I can't recall his name, but I remember that he was a weekend pastor, living in Atlanta and attending seminary at Interdenominational Theological Center. He told us about his participation in the March and chastised us by saying, "I didn't see any of you there." I remember resenting his statement, knowing that many in the group, myself included, were making personal sacrifices daily at home in LaGrange while he was only showing up on Sundays. I am embarrassed today by that reaction and the unconscious racism underlying it.

One day during this time, I received an anonymous communication criticizing my "race mixing." (I've always thought it was from the KKK church member who monitored the Council meetings, but I had no evidence of that.) He had copied (not an easy thing to do in 1965) an article quoting Methodist Bishop Kenneth Goodson. Bishop Goodson was one of those church leaders in Birmingham who had condemned Dr. Martin Luther King's civil rights activity, precipitating his famous *Letter from a Birmingham Jail*. The sender had written something to the effect, "Why can't you be like Bishop Goodson? People like you are destroying the Methodist Church." I did not particularly feel intimidated, but I realized, once again, how much more difficult it is to counter racism in a church and community when the highest church leaders fail to "have your back."

1965 was also the year that the Trustees of LaGrange College voted to give up its federal funding rather than agree to comply with the Civil Rights Act. The Chair of the Trustees was, of course, a Callaway executive and the son-in-law of Fuller Callaway himself. My "boss," Reynolds Greene, was also a trustee. Although I discussed the action of the Trustees with him, both before and after the vote, he never revealed to me what position he had taken in the discussions.

The consequence of the College's decision to maintain its white-only status was personified in one particular local high school student. King Harris was a high school senior anticipating graduation that year from the local high school for blacks. He was an active member of Warren Temple Methodist Church and a regular participant in our monthly Council meetings. He worked part-time for a local printer that, incidentally, printed the weekly bulletin for First Methodist Church. King wanted to be a minister but had very limited financial resources. Attending the local college, continuing his part-time job, and living at home seemed to be the perfect solution to his dilemma.

Toombs Kay, an ordained Methodist minister, religion professor at the College, and actively involved in both the Church and the Council, became his counselor and advocate in negotiating the admissions process. When his application was rejected by the College following the action of the Trustees, Toombs resigned his position in protest and took a position elsewhere.

Sometime early in the new year, Reynolds, the senior pastor, engaged me in a conversation about my plans for the next conference year, which would begin in mid-June. "Didn't I want to ask for an appointment to 'my own church?'" he asked. My response was, "No, I agreed to come for two years, and I expect to honor my commitment."

Our second conversation occurred a few days later. He told me there were people in the church who were unhappy with me and my ministry and warned that another year would not be an easy one for me. My response was, "No one has told me that they're unhappy with me or my ministry. Tell me who you're talking about so I can discuss it with them." He refused to share any name and suggested that my detractors were "too Christian" to criticize me directly and didn't want to hurt my feelings. I assured him that I had not become a minister to be "comfortable" and that I was sure I could deal with whatever unpleasantness might ensue.

Our final conversation was simply his announcement that he was requesting my reappointment, and I should talk to the district superintendent. Just as I was leaving, though, Reynolds offered me this "sage" advice: "Don't involve yourself with race in your new appointment. First, get the people to love you, and then you might be able to do so." That was not the lesson I took away from the experience. All my life, I had witnessed leaders of the church, clergy and lay, trying to get others to love them by avoiding race and other controversial issues. I was determined not to be that kind of leader, seeking to be loved, at whatever cost.

Here's what I learned from the LaGrange experience. Act boldly when confronting racism, making clear how your action is related to your faith and your core values. (I should have, for example, confronted the KKK church member who was monitoring attendance at the Council on Human Relations, told him what was going on inside, and invited him to come see for himself.) I never preached a sermon directly about race, believing that would have been "going too far." I should have. How are people going to change if they aren't shown a clear alternative to what they've always known.

Another lesson I learned in LaGrange is this. Don't enable a cover-up when an injustice is being done. If you're getting fired, let it be known you're getting fired. If "due process" has not been followed in making that determination, insist that the rules be followed and that you be afforded a chance to be heard. Reynolds dealt with my departure by inferring that I was leaving because I wanted "to have my own church." Almost everyone in the church assumed that to be the case; I didn't deny it. I met with no one but him to discuss my situation. I should have insisted that I be heard by the appropriate church body.

After I was gone, I learned from a friend what I believe to be the "real" reason for my firing. The friend reported that O.F.

.

Nixon, Jr., local businessman and church leader, had told Reynolds that he would withhold his substantial contribution to the church unless I was fired. (Ironically, Mr. Nixon was married to Lucy Lanier Nixon, heir to a substantial textile fortune and the source of his financial power. Lucy was the church organist and befriended us throughout my difficult year, even coming by on the day of our departure to bring us cookies.)

On my last Sunday I was scheduled to preach at the Sunday night service. (I was only allowed to preach on Sunday night, once a month. There had been one exception--Temperance Sunday, when the lay committee asked that I be the preacher.) I spent the afternoon at the church working on my sermon, and came home briefly to eat a light supper. Rose told me that there had been a telephone call earlier in the afternoon. The caller simply asked if I was preaching that night and inquired about the time of the service. She answered, "Yes, at 7:30." He said simply, "Thank you," and hung up. She told me she thought it was King Harris. Wow, I thought. Since no African American has ever attended a service at lily-white First Methodist, this could be interesting.

The Sunday night service had a simple order. When I was preaching, Reynolds would lead the rest of the service, beginning with hymn singing, a scripture reading, and a prayer. While we were singing the first hymn, King Harris and a teenage friend walked in and took a seat at the rear of the congregation. Very few people other than Reynolds and me were even aware of their presence. When Reynolds next stood, he did something I had never seen him do before on a Sunday night. He asked that the attendance registers be passed around, as he put it, "so we can know who you are." The service proceeded without incident and, while the last hymn was being sung, King and his friend quietly exited the church. That was the last time I saw him, since my move happened the next day…until ten years later.

In 1975 I was attending the North Georgia Conference session, now fully integrated. I had moved to Jacksonville the year before but continued to maintain my conference membership in North Georgia. As candidates for ordination were presented, much to my surprise and delight, I saw that King Harris was among the candidates. As soon as the session was over I rushed to find him and hear his story. Here's what had happened in the ten years intervening.

When he was refused admission to LaGrange College, having no money for attending college elsewhere, he joined the military. After completing his service, he enrolled at Edward Waters College, an African Methodist Episcopal school in Jacksonville, using his military educational benefits. After graduation he had enrolled at Interdenominational Theological Center in Atlanta, where he had just received his M.Div. degree.

I rejoiced with him about his accomplishments, delighting in his success and regretting the wrong that had been done to him in LaGrange. I wished, though, I had taken his hand and walked him over to Reynolds Greene, my former senior pastor, and to Waights Henry, still the LaGrange College President, both of whom were in attendance, asking, "Do you know who this is?" Perhaps, just perhaps, they might have said, "I'm sorry."

I can't conclude this chapter without including one other event of that last night in LaGrange. Rose left it out of her memoir, although, in publishing her work after her death in 2001, I decided to describe it. Here's my account.

After the Sunday evening service that "integrated" the church, I had gone with the youth group to someone's home for an after-church social. Rose drove home with Mark. (Bryan was staying with his grandparents while we packed our belongings for the move.) Arriving home, Rose parked in front of our house with the driver's side next to the curb. The street was on a small hill, and after she exited the car and was reaching inside to lift Mark out, the car began rolling backwards downhill. The wide-open door fortuitously caught on a large oak tree beside the curb. It was ripped off as Rose fell to the pavement. Mark was standing on the seat behind the steering wheel and must have grabbed the wheel, because the car swerved across the street and ran into the side of a car parked in front of a neighbor's house, stopping its movement. The neighbor was a member of our church, and the car that was hit belonged to the county sheriff. No one but Rose was hurt; her knees were scraped on the pavement.

Hearing Rose's screams, another neighbor who lived behind us came running to her rescue brandishing a pistol. So we left LaGrange with a big bang. A story in the newspaper the next day identified Mark as the driver of the car, so we have always insisted that he had his first driving accident at age four. (*A Passion for Justice*, p. 27)

Oakwood

Rose described my appointment to the Methodist Church in Oakwood, a small community in a rural area of Hall County outside Gainesville, a "punishment assignment." I don't think I shared her view. It was surely an "unfortunate assignment," though.

The two district superintendents who made the decision to send me there, John Tate (LaGrange) and Allen Oliver (Gainesville), were both friends of several years standing. I had been friends with their children during college days, and I believe they thought they were doing what was best both for me and for the church. In those days, there was no consultation with either the pastor or the church. Appointments were simply announced. (Rose would later help to change consultation practices in the 1970s when she was vice-chair of a national body appointed to study the itineracy.)

The Oakwood Church had never had a pastor with a seminary degree. Until recently, it had been one of multiple churches on a circuit with services only alternate Sundays. However, one of the state community colleges was scheduled to be built in the community, and it was hoped that I might be able to attract a more diverse membership. Most of the current members were blue collar workers in a local textile mill or at the GM plant in Atlanta, or small farmers. Many were part of a single extended family. Only one had a college education.

On my first Sunday, the district superintendent showed up to "introduce" me to the congregation. (This was not a usual custom and was another reason I felt he had my best interest at heart.) He proceeded to tell them about how much education I had and how fortunate they were to have me as their pastor. I wanted to crawl under a pew and hide. Before I had spoken my first word, he had erected a barrier between me and the people that I never managed to surmount.

The life of the Church, as they had experienced it, was centered in three services each week—Sunday morning, Sunday evening, and Wednesday night prayer meeting. The service centered on the sermon; all else was "preliminaries." I soon learned that sermons must be preached "from the heart," no manuscript. Families in the congregation attended five different camp meetings in the area each summer, and the evangelistic service of that tradition was their model. My predecessor preached "hellfire and damnation," with an altar call as the climax each week. Church was all about "getting saved." You can imagine how well I fit into their model and expectation.

Pastors in those days did a lot of visiting, and I was faithful in that task. People were cordial and kind, but did not have a clue about what kind of creature I was, perched on their front porch. I was always welcomed when I knocked on their doors, but they never seemed comfortable in my presence. They were not unlike many of my large extended family and the customers who shopped in my parents' store, with whom I conversed easily, but my role (and their expectations about that role) seemed to stand between us.

Although Rose had planned to be a full-time mother (Bryan and Mark were only one and four), she agreed to teach third grade when the local school principal pleaded, saying no one else with qualifications could be found. Furthermore, he promised to help arrange child care. Mark went to a pre-kindergarten program at the Presbyterian Church in Gainesville some days. Bryan received constant loving care from two elderly sisters from the community.

I can unequivocally say that this was the worst year of my life. I felt like a failure but had no idea what to do about it. The harder I worked on my three sermons each week, the less well they seemed to be received. The church was not interested in programs or education, two areas I knew something about. There were almost no weddings, funerals, sick calls, or counseling requested. I was, above all, bored.

Two monthly events would lift my spirits briefly. The first was the monthly meeting of the Ecumenical Ministerial Association in Gainesville, after which I usually had lunch with the Lutheran pastor and the Catholic priest. (The priest was desperately seeking help to understand what was happening to his world because of Vatican II.)

The other was the monthly gathering in Athens of a self-selected group of Methodist ministers (mostly mavericks like me) to discuss a new book suggested by an invited theology professor, who would join us for our discussion. It also functioned as a group "therapy" session, since I was not the only one struggling to keep his head above water in the parish. My seminary classmate, Ed Nelson, and I seemed frequently to be sharing similar experiences. (We continue to do so every summer at his home at Lake Junaluska.)

Surprisingly, race did not seem to be a front burner issue. The community was all-white, as were the school and the church, of course. I don't remember feeling constrained from talking about race. Our friend Olivia Masih from India spent several days with us at Christmas and even did a special presentation at the church. (Remember, I mentioned that she is dark-skinned.) She had grown up on a Methodist mission compound and told about her life there. (She wore her sari, of course.) She was very well received.

As spring approached and I contemplated another year there, I knew I was drowning, and I began to search for alternatives. I had the opportunity to be the appointed Conference Director of Youth Work, a job I knew well and would have loved doing, but it involved spending each summer at Camp Glisson. Remembering how unhappy Rose had been when we were there during my seminary years, I could not even consider it. I also had an interview for a staff position in Washington, D.C., with the General Board of Social and Economic Relations, but they were seeking someone with specialized knowledge I did not have.

My "salvation" arrived when the district superintendent threw me a lifeline by asking if I would be interested in a position as Wesley Foundation Director in Milledgeville, Georgia. I had no idea what that might be like, but, desperate to escape my situation before I "went under for the last time," I said, "Yes."

Part VI   Milledgeville

I've written elsewhere that I didn't discover what I wanted to be when I grew up until I was thirty-one (the summer I moved to Milledgeville). I soon learned that campus ministry was indeed my niche, and continued to spend myself in that endeavor for forty more years. I thrived on the openness to new ideas and the willingness to question old ones that the college environment encouraged. I was energized by the demand to create ministry activity that was both faithful and fresh, unburdened by "the way we've always done it." And perhaps most of all, I loved being free to foster community open to everybody, "free to be, you and me."

Rose, Mark, Bryan, and I moved into a very small apartment inside the Wesley Foundation House, a Methodist student center in the midst of the campus of (then) Woman's College of Georgia. When you walked in the front door (always open, at least until 11:00 p.m.), a door to the right led to our apartment. A door to the left opened into a pool room, frequented most often by students from Georgia Military College, a municipal prep school and junior college a few blocks away on the grounds of the old State Capitol. A short flight of stairs led down to a lounge and meeting room, with a TV, record player, and large kitchen (many meals were prepared there), opening onto an outdoor patio.

Directly behind us was one of the College's residence halls. On our north side lived Colquitt Koepps, probably in her 80s, in the home built by her great-grandfather in the 1840s after leaving office as Governor. Directly across the street on the corner was the Binyon House, a newer mansion built in the ante-bellum style. In the block just north of there, visible from our front door, were the former Governor's Mansion (now the home of the College President), the Cline House (a childhood home of Flannery O'Connor, where her mother still lived), the First Methodist Church, and an unoccupied residence hall that would become the first men's dormitory a year later when the College became co-educational.

In addition to the two colleges already mentioned, Milledgeville was the home of Milledgeville State Hospital, at the time the only mental health facility in the State, with a population of

18,000. Their Affiliate Program in Psychiatric Nursing provided a quarter-long clinical experience for nursing students from hospital-based programs throughout the State. The Wesley Foundation provided a dinner and program for these students weekly.

In the mid-60s, Milledgeville was a very small town of the old South. It had been the State Capitol at the time of the Civil War, its streets lined with many magnificent homes spared by Sherman in his march to the sea. It was the county seat of Baldwin County, whose population was equally divided between blacks and whites, still living with the rigid segregation of Jim Crow.

I remember going to the local movie theater to see *In the Heat of the Night*. Whites sat downstairs, and blacks sat in the balcony. When the Mississippi sheriff, played by Rod Steiger, would score a point, there would be loud laughter from downstairs, followed by a roar from the balcony when the New York detective, played by Sydney Poitier, responded in kind. (The theater was soon desegregated after many white students, discovering that a lower admission was being charged for the balcony, began sitting there.)

If I had been looking for a site to study racial change in the South, I could not have found a more ideal setting than Milledgeville. The "Southern way of life" was firmly ensconced there. Yet, multiple forces were converging to produce change, led by growing pressure to enforce the proscriptions of Brown v. Board of Education.

If I had been looking for a mentor to teach me about racism in all its dimensions, I could not have found anyone better able to open my eyes, point my feet, and hold my hand than Charlie Alston, Chaplain at the State Hospital. More about him later.

If I had been looking for a group of people with whom to share a journey toward racial justice, I could not have found a more caring, committed community than the multi-faceted one that emerged in Milledgeville.

Woman's College was technically integrated. The first black student, Celestine Hill, had been admitted in 1964. Celestine, a local student living on a farm outside of town, became our friend and told us this story about her family. Her grandfather was a Scotsman who married a black woman. Somehow, they were able to continue to live in the area (although interracial marriage was forbidden by Georgia law), perhaps because he owned considerable land. He also owned the building housing a large drug store in the middle of town operated by Culver Kidd, State Senator and former Lieutenant Governor, the most powerful political figure in the area. Celestine's father inherited the downtown property, and consequently became Senator Kidd's landlord. Celestine seemed to enjoy that relationship. Celestine would sometimes sit on the floor in our living room, usually with Maggie Blackwood, the white Y-director at the College, "educating" us about our new hometown and its racial realities. (Celestine and Maggie spent the summer of 1967 doing civil rights work in the Southwest Georgia Project of Student Interracial Ministries.)

When we arrived in 1966, Celestine and Lucretia Coleman, another local student, were the only black students enrolled. (More about Lucretia later.) When we left three years later, there were about fifty or so, several of them living on campus.

After our first year, with increased numbers and the first males in the College's history, the Wesley Foundation became the gathering place for the black student population.

I'm not sure exactly why that happened. One reason probably was that, in a town still barring blacks from public places, they had almost nowhere else they could go. Another probable reason was that, most weeks, other groups that included local blacks met at our building. (More about those later.) Our openness to others had already been demonstrated by a Coffee House (yes, it was the 60s) that we sponsored on Saturday nights. I prefer, though, to think that the primary reason was that we warmly welcomed all people.

On weekend nights, especially, the sounds of "soul" music floated out of the Center and drifted into the surrounding antebellum houses built by Southern aristocrats. White students were there, too, enjoying a setting where blacks and whites could be together on an equal footing—a new experience for most of them. I'm sure there were other white students who thought we were an abomination. I was criticized, of course, for "excluding" them.

Weekly Recreation Program for State Hospital Patients

One of the programs I inherited when I arrived at the Wesley Foundation had been initiated by the previous Director, Bert Gratigny. First, I should share a little background on Milledgeville State Hospital. Until the early 1960s, the Hospital had been largely custodial, offering no treatment, simply warehousing whoever was "committed" there by the County Ordinary. (Think of it as the institution depicted in the disturbing movie of 1948 *The Snake Pit.*) Established in 1837 as the "State Lunatic, Idiot, and Epileptic Asylum," it was the only mental health facility in the state.

In 1959, *Atlanta Journal* investigative reporter Jack Nelson wrote a scathing expose describing conditions there. Betty Vandiver, wife of the Governor, took up the cause, and some things began to change. By 1966, when I arrived in Milledgeville, great progress had been made, but most long-term patients still received little or no treatment.

Our program brought together a group of female patients, transported weekly to our Student Center, and a group of students, many of whom were recreation majors, for a time of fun and games. Most of the patients had been confined to the Hospital for many years. I especially remember two strong women who had somehow survived the years of neglect. One had a hideous birth mark covering much of her face. Since it was frightening to look at her, "society" had locked her away, out of sight. A second, according to the story I was told, had murdered her father after enduring years of abuse. To avoid dealing with her as a criminal, she had "mercifully" been shut up in the Hospital for years.

While we could not provide a remedy for the horrific situation these women found themselves in, we did provide a respite—and an amazing opportunity for students to experience aspects of life hidden from most of us.

Concern

The two experiences that provided the most significant learning about racism I had yet known were not a result of my own initiative. The first began in the unlikeliest of places—the local ministerial association. Surprisingly, in a community still rigidly divided by race, the Baldwin County Ministerial Association was integrated. (I suspect that was largely because the two remarkable black chaplains who had recently been hired by the State Hospital, Charlie Alston and Payton Cook, just showed up.)

The speaker that day was named Roger but I can't even recall his last name now. (He moved away not long after this occasion.) He was a minister but was currently employed as a social worker. He really "laid it on us" that day. After describing in graphic detail some of the realities of poverty in our community, he challenged us to "do something" about it.

Somehow, at the conclusion of the meeting, three of us ended up as a task force to plan a response—Milton Murray, rector of St. Stephen's Episcopal Church, Charlie Alston, and me. Charlie and I persuaded Milton to be our chair, but Charlie was really our leader. He knew what needed to be done and how to do it. Milton was our public face, giving us respectability and managing the "heat" that would eventually ensue. I was the work horse.

The organization that grew out of that "call to conscience" became a grassroots movement for change, decades overdue but ready to be born. When I moved away three years later, there were a hundred members, equally divided, black and white. A year after that, it became an affiliate of the Southern Christian Leadership Conference.

We called ourselves Concern. Meetings were held at the Wesley Foundation House, causing the movement to be identified with our ministry. Remarkably, concerned citizens from both the white and black communities showed up for our open, public meetings from the very beginning. They came from the churches, the colleges, and the State Hospital staff primarily. The first project undertaken was a Clothes Closet (who could object to that?), and the Catholic priest offered space in their Parish House to locate it.

School Lunches

Rose, in her memoir, describes how our next project was born. "One muggy, August afternoon," she wrote, "a group of us were sitting in an upstairs room of the Parish House mending children's clothes for distribution before school started. The sun slanted through the windows spotlighting layers of dusty air. One of the women was old Mrs. Brown, who had been a teacher at the black elementary school for at least thirty years. Her husband was the longtime president of the local NAACP chapter.

"When the conversation lagged, Mrs. Brown sighed deeply and said: "The worst thing about going back to school is deciding who gets a free lunch."

"'What do you mean, Mrs. Brown," I asked innocently. "Doesn't every child who qualifies receive a free lunch?"

"No, the way it works is each teacher is allowed five free lunches, and we have to decide who in our class gets to eat lunch that day. It always breaks my heart that some children are going hungry."

"The white women sitting there were stunned. We knew that the federal free lunch program provided for any child who met the criteria. What could be the problem?" (*A Passion for Justice*, pp. 31-32)

After doing some research, we discovered that the local school system had failed to request federal funds sufficient to feed all the children needing assistance in the black schools. We also learned that it was too late to request additional funds for the current school year. Dismayed, we recruited a task force to meet with Frank Lawrence, the school superintendent, to see what could be done. Charlie and I were on the task force, along with Levi Swinger, a business administrator at the State Hospital, and Alice Goddard, recently retired from the professional staff of the Religious Education Association, an arm of the National Council of Churches in New York.

Our meeting with Superintendent Lawrence was cordial. When we asked about children who were not receiving free lunches but were eligible, he said that surely a few probably "fell through the cracks." Whenever that happened, someone would usually step up to be that child's sponsor. We made it clear that we expected the school system to request enough federal funds for the next year. In the meantime, we pledged, we would find sponsors for all the children who have "fallen through the cracks."

I'm sure that he expected us to identify a handful of children, provide sponsors, and then forget about the whole situation. Rather, we proceeded to survey every teacher in every school, asking how many free lunches they had available and the names of children needing but not receiving them. Our final count was over 900 children. Simultaneously, we launched a public campaign, led by Alice, including human interest stories featured in the local newspaper. We managed to get a sponsor for every single child, despite a successful power play by the embarrassed school system eventually blocking our newspaper coverage.

Again, we met with the Superintendent along with his Deputy to insist that adequate federal funds be requested for the next school year. This time, cordiality had vanished, and we were met with outright hostility. Here are three comments I recall from that meeting, whether made by the School Superintendent or his Deputy I can't be sure. Questioning our numbers of children needing free lunches, gathered directly from the classroom teachers, he said, "You know you just can't trust black teachers to be honest." Another statement: "I don't know why you're so concerned. Those people aren't used to eating three meals a day anyway." And the most outrageous comment of all: "If it hadn't been for Roosevelt's New Deal, these people would have died out during the Depression, and we wouldn't have this problem today."

Clearly, more fundamental change was needed. When we investigated the "system," we learned that the Superintendent was appointed by the School Board. The School Board was selected by the Grand Jury. The Grand Jury was presided over by the Superior Court Judge. The Superior Court Judge was George Lawrence, the brother of the School Superintendent. It was clear that, if we were to succeed in getting the attention of the school system, political change would be required.

I remember vividly a meeting Charlie set up with Senator Culver Kidd. I'm not sure who all was involved, but I remember it began with a short speech by Charlie reminding Senator Kidd that he had been elected, in part, because the well-organized black vote had supported him. Blacks were half of the total population in Baldwin County. Although many were not registered (more about that later), they still constituted a substantial voting bloc. Being an astute politician, Senator Kidd agreed to introduce legislation to create an elected school board. While it did not happen during my time in Milledgeville, the legislation eventually was enacted.

The "school lunch struggle" opened my eyes to so many realities. I understood in a more profound and personal way the depth of racism all around me. I recognized how dehumanizing our system, how grotesque our prejudices, how entrenched our injustices really are.

I experienced as well how one thing leads to another that, in turn, leads to still another, and, before you know it, you have risked more than you intended. Who (except probably Mrs. Brown) could have imagined that sitting together mending used clothes for needy school children would result in legislation to change the governance of the school system. Who (except probably Charlie) could have imagined that simply trying to get available federal funds to feed hungry children would be so controversial.

I also experienced the exhilaration of knowing that my efforts, joined with those of others, especially when there are substantial risks, can truly make a difference. And, finally, I experienced the "beloved community" that emerges from such an endeavor.

Black History

Another Concern undertaking took me by surprise. Early on we identified a deep hunger in both the white and black communities for learning about black American history. A white history professor agreed to prepare a series of lectures, although he had not taught such a course before. We purchased copies of a popular text, arranged use of the College's facilities, and publicized the opportunity widely in the community. Nearly a hundred people, as I recall, showed up for our weekly gatherings at the College. Until then, I was barely aware of my/our profound ignorance of the substantial contributions black Americans had made to our national life and culture. I learned as well the urgency for encouraging black pride.

Voter Registration

Prior to the 1968 elections, Concern decided to address the sparsity of black registered voters in Baldwin County. I don't remember the numbers, but, primarily because of past and present discrimination, too few blacks were registered. Consequently, despite being half the population, blacks held no public office. So we set out in teams of two, one black, one white, to knock on doors and get folks registered. I had the good fortune to be teamed with Payton Cook, State Hospital chaplain and friend.

When we found someone who wanted to register, we would take them down to the registration office immediately if they were willing. One of us would ask the clerk for a registration card and assist the potential voter in completing it. We soon discovered an illegal practice. Registered voters were not supposed to be identified by race. However, Baldwin County was circumventing that law, we discovered, by giving blacks an off-white registration card while whites were registered on a white card. We were unwittingly disrupting that practice when I would ask for a card and use it for registering a black voter.

Peonage

Another experience I shared with Payton Cook grew out of an incident at the Clothes Closet. In assisting a large black family in selecting clothes, one of our Concern members had observed that the family appeared to fear the white man who had brought them there. They had come from another part of the state to work on his farm. Our member suspected that they might be working there against their will.

Payton and I agreed to pay a visit to the family and offer assistance if needed. We drove out to the farm after Payton finished work at the Hospital late one afternoon. We managed to find the shack in which they were all living without encountering the "boss." Because of their fearfulness, we were never able to be sure that they were living in peonage (a state of near slavery, prohibited by law, where a laborer is bound to personal service to work off a debt). We suspected it was so. We assured them that they had a right to leave at any time they wished to do so. We further assured them that our organization was willing to assist them in doing so if, at any time, they desired our help. We never heard from them again while I was still in the area.

Two More "Revelations"

I can't remember how I happened to be a part of this conversation, but I'm glad I was. A black woman who was actively involved with our Concern group, (I regretfully have forgotten her name, so I will use a fictitious one) Sara Jones, had been involved in a minor traffic accident near downtown. The other car involved was driven by a white woman. The accident was clearly the fault of the white woman but both had been given traffic citations. When the two women appeared before City Court, Judge Joe Dukes called Sara Jones by her first name, but addressed the white woman as Mrs.

Incensed but unable to express that in Court, Mrs. Jones had shared the experience with Chaplain Charlie Alston (see above), who in turn shared it with me. Judge Dukes was a member of the Methodist Church and a member of the Wesley Foundation Board as well. Chaplain Alston made an appointment to speak with Judge Dukes and asked me to accompany him.

At the appointment, Chaplain Alston recounted the incident, and "explained" to Judge Dukes that calling Mrs. Jones by her first name in that circumstance was unacceptable and hurtful. Judge Dukes defended his behavior by saying that Mrs. Jones had worked for his family, and he considered her a friend. Chaplain Alston "explained" the difference between personal settings and public ones, and made it clear that, if Judge Dukes expected to continue to receive the support of black voters in the next election, he needed to change his behavior.

Clearly, the Judge's form of address was racial discrimination, even if innocently spoken. This incident underscored what I think I may have already known. In public settings, one should never refer to blacks without using the appropriate title, regardless of friendship and even if non-blacks are referred to by their first names. This "custom" in the black community should be understood and honored.

Another revelation occurred on a Sunday morning at Flagg Chapel Baptist Church, an historically black church, two blocks south of the Student Center. I had been asked to preach there, and Rose and the boys, ages seven and four, accompanied me.

I was sitting up front, of course, and they were seated in the center section, three or four pews from the front. I was surprised that communion was being celebrated, since white Baptists are usually "exclusive" about participation in that rite. Unlike Methodists, the communion elements are passed down the pews. As I sat watching, it dawned on me that Rose would unthinkingly encourage Mark and Bryan to participate as was our custom. As they each took the bread and container of grape juice, I could almost hear a gasp in the congregation. It was definitely not the custom in this Baptist Church for children to partake of the communion elements.

Of course, no one said anything then or afterwards. Everyone was gracious and welcoming. While we had no intention of offending anyone, we had certainly committed a gaffe. I learned anew how important it is to be aware of and honor the customs and traditions of others, especially if their customs and traditions have not always been honored in the past.

A Disturbing Conversation

One afternoon I was picking up Bryan from his preschool class at Peabody. While waiting for the activity to be over, I had a disturbing conversation with the mother of one of his classmates. She was a black social worker at the State Hospital and had been involved in some of the Concern meetings and activities. I hardly knew her, but she presumed she "knew" me (and probably did).

She began to tell me how wrong it was that "all you white folks" are the dominant leaders in these programs for "us black folks." "We should be the leaders," she insisted. At the time I was slated to become the Chair of Concern at the end of the school year. I can't remember how I responded at the time, but as I began writing this memoir, the incident popped into my consciousness. I suspect I responded defensively. She was right, of course.

Tutoring Program

Another transforming experience began one Sunday after church in a conversation with Bobbie Crittenden. Bobbie had been our son Mark's kindergarten teacher at the Peabody Demonstration School at the College. Beginning in the summer of 1967, though, she had taken on a special assignment as part of the county school system's desegregation plan. She was teaching a special class of kindergartners at the all-black Carver School, hoping to prepare them for a successful integrated classroom experience. She had learned that most of her kids needed special help and challenged me to recruit college students for that task. When I presented the opportunity to Wesley students, they enthusiastically agreed.

For the next two years, we would bring the twenty or so kids to the Wesley Foundation House weekly for "tutoring." We had an equal number of college student volunteers to provide a one-on-one experience. We provided enrichment activities of all sorts, from simply reading to them to field trips. Frequently we served a meal.

I visited the homes of many of the kids. What an education! Most lived in poverty beyond anything I had ever imagined. Some had no running water. Their electricity might be simply a single light bulb hanging from a cord in the ceiling. I remember that one kid's family lost all they had when their house burned, a common experience in their slum neighborhood.

It was well known in the community that most of the poor housing was owned by two widows—one white and one black. The white owner was "Miss Tillie" Kidd, mother of Senator Culver Kidd, who would drive to each house to collect the rent in a Lincoln Town Car with her pistol on the seat beside her. You never wanted to sit behind her at the Methodist Church on Sunday because she was quite tall and always wore a huge picture hat.

The black owner was Mrs. Boddie, whose late husband had been a doctor. She was also the grandmother of Michael Boddie, our son Mark's classmate in the first grade, the first year of integration.

I'll tell only two of the many stories emanating from this project. Hoping to make Christmas that year really special, I decided to invite Chaplain Payton Cook to be Santa Claus at the holiday party we were planning for the kids. Payton and I had become friends through Concern, and, since he was huge, at least 6'6", with an outgoing personality, I thought he would be perfect. I thought, too, having a black Santa Claus would be special.

He loved the idea and readily agreed. However, when he showed up, all dressed up, the kids didn't believe he was the real thing. They had never seen a black Santa Claus before and felt they had been short-changed.

The other story is about one particular kid—Michael Simmons. Michael was one of eleven children living in abject poverty just a few short blocks from the campus. He had an electrifying personality and, despite the deprivations of his life, was extremely enterprising. We learned, for example, that he had collected pecans from the city park and sold them to buy himself shoes. Even with the best efforts of Ms. Crittenden and our student "tutors," Michael could still not read when he reached the second grade. Fortunately, Ms. Selma Erwin became his teacher. (She was our son Mark's teacher that year as well.)

Ms. Selma, the finest teacher I've been privileged to know, took on Michael as her special project. He had somehow managed to get a paper route, and since she knew almost everybody in town, Ms. Selma asked several of his customers to write him notes. Although he had not been motivated before to learn to read (his parents were likely illiterate), he would bring these notes to Ms. Selma, seeking her help in understanding and responding to them. After weeks of "correspondence," Michael became a reader.

Here's the sad part of the story, though. Several years after we moved away from Milledgeville, we learned that Michael told Ms. Selma (who continued to be his special friend) that he wanted to set himself on fire. Horrified, she asked, "Why,

Michael?" "Because," he said, "the scars would make my skin white, and then I could have things like the white folks do."

These two stories still haunt me. I have no doubt that our tutorial project enriched the lives of these special kids in many, many ways. I still wonder, though, about what damage we caused by unconsciously identifying whiteness with the source of good fortune.

Flannery O'Connor

In case you are not acquainted with her, Flannery O'Connor is a Southern Gothic writer now taught in most American literature classes. She is likely the most famous Milledgeville personage of all time. She spent her teen years there, graduated from the College, and returned there to live and write in the final years of her short life. She died in 1964 at her mother's farm, Andalusia, a few miles outside town, just two years before I moved there. She was only thirty-nine years old, and suffered from disseminated lupus, the same disease that claimed the life of her father at an early age.

Rose and I had read her works, and I decided to use her recently-published final book of short stories, *Everything That Rises Must Converge*, as the "text" for a Sunday school class I taught for college students at First Methodist Church. I found her orthodox Catholic theology challenging (if not appealing), and I was fascinated by the characters she created to inhabit her stories. Even today, I believe it was a good way to learn about the people and the religion of my new community.

Flannery's characters were really in-depth caricatures. (She had been a cartoonist for the College newspaper during her student days.) I remember a visit with Ms. Turner, the widow of a local dentist and a member of the Methodist Church who lived up the street from us. She was quite intelligent, had known Flannery, and continued to be a good friend of Flannery's mother, Regina. She told us that most all the local people were utterly bewildered by Flannery's writings. "Where in the world did she get her characters?" they wondered. Ms. Turner then proceeded to identify a number of them for us.

Weeks later, Rose came home from her first visit to our local doctor, Charles Fulghum. She exclaimed, "I've just been in one of Flannery's stories." Dr. Fulghum was indeed Flannery's doctor, we discovered, and his waiting room was clearly the scene of perhaps her finest story, "Revelation."

I include this reflection here because I continue to be indebted to Flannery and her insights into the South, its religion, and its culture. Flannery writes frequently about race. (How can you write about the South without doing so?) Critics continue to debate whether or not she was a racist. My answer is, "Of course, she was. You don't grow up in the old South without acquiring 'it' along with an accent." Her racism, though, did not prevent her seeing the racism that permeated the world around her—and helping her readers see it as well.

I'm also indebted to Flannery for helping me be more self-discerning about "do-gooders." (I lay claim to the designation myself.) Her story "The Lame Shall Enter First" continues to cause me to examine my life and my motivations more deeply.

Family Matters

Our sons, Mark and Bryan, were five and two, respectively, when we moved to Milledgeville. They had already lived in three different houses (not including Mark's summer cabin experience). Now we were moving them into a tiny apartment with hardly any lawn inside a Center with a constant flow of students. They were also tagged with that infamous label "PK" (Preacher's Kid).

Rose's nephew, Allen Lowe (just a month younger than Mark), was spending most of that first summer with us while his parents were in France. On our first Sunday we dressed everybody up to walk the block to the Church. Of course, Allen stepped in a mud puddle before we left and had to go back and change. We learned from Mark and Allen's Sunday school teacher later that they had introduced themselves as "the new bad boys who'd just come to town." (I think they must have been quoting a Western movie.)

Soon after our move, Bryan was diagnosed as having calcium deposits on his knees (knock-kneed) and advised to wear steel braces preventing his bending his knees. For several months, his activities were extremely limited. He spent a lot of time listening to recordings. He especially loved Marlo Thomas's "Free to Be, You and Me" album.

In the fall, Mark began kindergarten at the Peabody Demonstration School on the other side of the campus, under the tutelage of Bobbie Crittenden (see above). He soon had a best friend, Shaun Hannon, whose father was a child psychologist at the State Hospital. Bryan was an occasional playmate of Shaun's sister as well.

Head Start

Near the end of the school year, we learned that the local Head Start program, designed for preschoolers needing special preparation for first grade, was in trouble. All the children enrolled were black. The parents of eligible white children were unwilling to let them participate, and the federal funding was consequently threatened. The director asked if we would allow Mark to attend. Believing in the importance of the program and thinking that Mark would benefit, we agreed. His best friend, Shaun, enrolled, too, as did a girl from his kindergarten class. They were the only white kids involved but were enough to keep the program funded.

As Rose described in her memoir, "Mark seemed to enjoy the experience. (I'd be curious to hear his present memories of that summer.) I remember that he was fascinated by the food served, especially yellow grits. One day he came home and asked why we never had 'possum to eat. (Apparently 'possum was a special treat for some of his new classmates.) The fact that all the teachers and almost all the students were black never seemed to enter his consciousness." (*A Passion for Justice*, pp. 34-35)

The following school year was the first year of desegregation in the Baldwin County schools. The "freedom of choice" plan was beginning with only pre-school and first grade. I'm not sure how many black kids (not many) were in Mark's class at Peabody. I know that at least one, Michael Boddie, became his good friend. Michael's father was a doctor. (His grandmother was the slum landlady mentioned above.) Their teacher was white. Rose and Ms. Boddie were the room mothers.

PTA Luncheon

Following custom, the Peabody PTA planned a luncheon honoring the teachers and room mothers at the end of the year. As always, the luncheon was scheduled to be held at the Country Club, where blacks were not welcomed. When Ms. Kennedy, Mark's teacher, informed Rose that Ms. Boddie was not being invited, Rose telephoned the PTA president in protest, requesting that the luncheon be relocated. When she refused, Rose said she would not attend, promising to inform others, who would likely not attend as well. The PTA president hung up without saying goodbye. A few days later, though, she called to say that the luncheon had been moved to a local restaurant where all could attend. Rose attended, but Ms. Boddie did not. Rose was not invited to be a room mother the next year. I'm not sure about Ms. Boddie.

Both Mark and Bryan continued at Peabody during the years we were in Milledgeville. The school provided an excellent educational experience, but unfortunately that experience was available only to a few. Their classes were all integrated, but included only a few black kids. We were pleased that their schooling, almost from the beginning, could be interracial, even if only in a token way.

The Barton Trust: Neil Jen

Ma Barton (see above) continued to offer us opportunities to expand our world and enrich our lives through international friendships. She had been introduced to Neil Jen by an Atlanta pastor, and he soon became part of her large international family. Neil was from Taiwan (originally, though, from Mainland China). He was enrolled in the Masters in Library

Science program at Atlanta University, the historically black graduate school. When he completed his degree, she used her long-time "connections" at the Woman's College to help him secure a job there. She then passed him on to us.

Neil's wife Lilly and three-year-old son Len Chen, who had remained in Taiwan while he earned his degree, soon joined him. They enriched our life experience in countless ways. Lilly spoke little English and Len Chen (whom they began to call Jim), none. Soon after their arrival, Neil and Lilly left Len Chen with us while they attended a reception at the home of the College President. I asked Neil what he would say if he needed to use the bathroom (all the Chinese I considered necessary to know.) Bryan and Len Chen played together happily, each constantly chattering in his own language, the other seeming to understand perfectly. After a year or so, the Jens moved to Salisbury State College in Maryland, where Neil spent the rest of his career. Now living in retirement in Gaithersburg, Maryland, they continue to be part of my extended family.

The Barton Trust: Lucretia Coleman

Lucretia Coleman, the second black student to enroll at the College, presented us with an opportunity to expand the reach of the Barton Trust beyond the international student community. Early in her senior year, Lucretia approached me seeking financial assistance. A so-called "day" student, Lucretia lived with her mother and sister in a small, wooden house near the campus. They had few financial resources, but she had managed to scrape together the funds for the first three years. Now, getting close to graduation, she was afraid she would not be able to finish without additional financial help. Ma and the other Board members gladly agreed to expand our reach to include black students like Lucretia. More than anything, she needed the reassurance that, if she ran out of funds, someone would be there to help. As I recall, she only needed assistance in buying her books.

One afternoon in late winter, Lucretia showed up at my office in tears. She had just received her assignment for student teaching, the last hurdle before graduation, and learned some disturbing news. Expecting to receive an assignment in Fulton County along with all the other student teachers, she had made arrangements to share affordable housing with some other students in that locale. However, she had been assigned to an all-black school in another county. Even more upsetting was the fact that the assigned K-12 school had only one class in her business education field—typing. I assured her that I would see what could be done to alter that.

I was slightly acquainted with the professor who headed the student teaching program; he was an active member of the Methodist Church. So I called and asked if I could come see him. Walking across campus to his office, I decided to stop on the way at the office of the Registrar, Linton Cox, who happened to be Chair of the Campus Ministry Board. (I sensed there might be resistance, and I wanted him to know in advance what I was about to do.)

When I sat down with the professor, I began by explaining my relationship with Lucretia as a financial sponsor for her education. I acknowledged that it must be difficult to place the first black student in this time of transition, but I explained how distressing the assignment was for Lucretia and asked that an alternative be found. He was incensed, insisting that her assignment had nothing to do with her race, and declared that it was too late to change it.

After making clear that his response was unacceptable, I left, promising to pursue the matter further. On my way back to the office, I again stopped at Linton's office to report what had ensued. Later the same day, Linton called to let me know that he had just come from a meeting called by the College President and that Lucretia's assignment had been changed.

Why? Perhaps it was simply a decision "higher up" to do the right thing. I suspect, though, it was a realization that, because of my connection with Concern, the discrimination practiced on Lucretia would become public and controversial. Concern had truly become a political force to be reckoned with in the Baldwin County community.

After completing her degree, Lucretia supported her sister's college education. She then earned a Ph.D. degree at the University of Tennessee, and returned to teach at the College. I must tell one more story, though, involving Lucretia.

The College Alumni Association traditionally hosted the college faculty annually at a luncheon held at the Country Club (yes, the same place featured in the PTA story above). When Lucretia returned to give the faculty a little "color," the Country Club still excluded blacks. Unbelievably, so I've been told, the Alumni Association continued to hold its luncheon there. Lucretia was just not invited.

The Funeral of Dr. Martin Luther King, Jr.

When Dr. Martin Luther King, Jr., was assassinated on April 3, 1968, many students, both black and white, gathered at the Center to express their grief. We immediately began to make plans to go to his funeral in Atlanta, only seventy miles away. Most of the black students were determined to make the trip. Two female white students, our most recent Student Presidents, especially wanted to be included. However, the College would not permit resident students to travel out of town without permission from their parents, and their parents would not give their consent.

So, on April 8, eleven black students and I made the trip to Atlanta together. We parked halfway between Morehouse College, site of the service for the general public, and Ebenezer Baptist Church on Auburn Avenue, site of the service for invited guests. We joined thousands of mourners outside Ebenezer, listening to the service over loudspeakers and waiting for the march to Morehouse to begin.

When the service was over, the dignitaries poured out of the church behind the wooden coffin that was placed on a wagon behind a team of mules. As they marched past us, I remember watching Richard Nixon (not yet President) walking beside basketball legend Wilt Chamberlain, whose whole upper body seemed to float above the crowd. Bobby Kennedy attracted applause from the bystanders as he passed by. Noticeable by their absence were President Lyndon B. Johnson and Georgia Governor Lester Maddox.

When the church had emptied, the students and I joined the masses in the march to Morehouse, maybe two miles away. Our route took us by Wesley Memorial Methodist Church, headquarters for the North Georgia Conference and scene of some of my earliest interracial experiences and my most public witness. I knew that the Methodist Bishop and his District Superintendents were meeting there that day to make decisions about pastoral appointments, carrying on business as usual while the world around them was in turmoil over the killing of the century's greatest prophet and peacemaker. I wept that day, not just for Dr. King but for the Church I loved as well.

The outdoor service on the huge lawn at Morehouse is somewhat a blur in my memory. I have images, though, both visual and auditory. I remember the sounds of Mahalia Jackson singing "Precious Lord, Take My Hand." I remember the eloquent and moving eulogy by Dr. Benjamin Mays, Morehouse President and leader of the Atlanta black community. But, most of all, I remember the faces of those gathered there, most of them black, and the broken hearts they displayed.

There was to be a memorial service in Milledgeville that night, to be held, remarkably, in the County Courthouse. I so wanted to be there, but there was no way I could do so. Getting back to our cars and out of Atlanta was a nightmare. Rose, though, who had stayed in Milledgeville, was determined to go. Frantically searching for childcare, she tried all her usual babysitters, mostly local high school or college students. None of them were available, primarily because their parents were afraid for their safety if they were out on that particular night. (The white communities all over the country expected riots, and they did occur in some communities, although neither in Milledgeville nor Atlanta.) Finally, Jane Murray, the wife of the Episcopal rector, volunteered to keep our sons with her daughter while Rose attended.

That week was Holy Week, and our local Methodist church was having a revival. I was able to survive in Milledgeville and other conservative communities partly because I was very attentive to and supportive of local church activities. On the morning after the King funeral, bright and early, I was at the breakfast that was a part of the revival schedule. I had been badly sunburned the day before, and my face was a bright red. Two dear ladies sitting across from me at the breakfast asked if I had been vacationing in Florida. "No, I replied. "I was attending the memorial service for Dr. King." That ended the conversation."

An Interracial Romance

Susan Yandle was the President of our Wesley Student Council at the time of the King assassination and one of the white students unable to go to the funeral because her parents would not give their permission. In most ways, she fit the stereotype of the all-American girl—blonde, blue-eyed, attractive, vivacious. She had led our annual Student Day service at First Methodist Church a few months earlier and had wowed the congregation with her charismatic leadership. Henry Davis was another student active in the Wesley program. He was handsome, blessed with a winning personality, and an enthusiastic participant in many of our activities. Susan and Henry had begun to date, a not uncommon occurrence among our flock. There was only one problem; Henry was black.

One morning I received a call from Bruce Yandle, Susan's father. Incidentally, he was business manager of the state-wide

Methodist publication *Wesleyan Christian Advocate* produced in Macon. He was in distress because Susan had told him about her relationship with Henry. He thought that Susan trusted and respected me, and he was seeking my help in convincing her to break off the relationship. My response was to acknowledge his concern for Susan and his legitimate worry about the difficulty of an interracial relationship. However, I made it clear to him that I viewed the students with whom I worked as maturing adults, responsible for making their own decisions. While I welcomed opportunities to "counsel" them, I would never tell them what they should do or not do. I tried to assure him that I viewed Susan and Henry as among the most level-headed students with whom I worked and believed they were not taking the difficulties of their relationship lightly. As you might suspect, he did not find my response adequate.

I don't remember ever having a conversation with Susan about my conversation with her father. I would certainly not have initiated such a conversation. The spring semester was soon over, and Susan did not return in the fall.

Church Politics

At about this point in my story, if you have had experience with church politics, you may be asking, "How were you able to keep your job while engaging in these high-risk ministries?" Here's what I've concluded.

My primary accountability was to an independent Wesley Foundation Board. They met, I think, quarterly. Two Board Chairs served during my three-year tenure. Turner Farmer, a professor at the College, the first year, and Linton Cox, College Registrar, during my last two years. Both were active members of First Methodist Church, highly respected both on campus and in the congregation. Neither would have been involved in many of the activities they were called on to defend, but they respected my calling and always "had my back."

The local pastor (Charlie Middlebrooks my first year, Rembert Sisson my last two years) was a particularly critical member of the Board. I had known both Charlie and Rembert earlier, and their personal support was unfailing, although I'm sure they sometimes "took heat" because of it.

The Board also included assorted members of the local church and college community, including our Student President, along with special friends of the ministry from throughout the two Methodist conferences (just the white ones, I regret to say).

The Executive Secretary of the Georgia Commission on Higher Education, Dan Brewster, was an ex-officio member, always present and always more cautious than the local folks. (His "timidity" was largely, I think, because his agency was responsible for raising money from the churches to support all the colleges and campus ministries throughout the state.) Although I'm sure the District Superintendent was an ex-officio member, he was located in Augusta, almost a hundred miles away, further than Atlanta. Since I can't even remember who he was, his involvement must have been minimal.

I was diligent about keeping the Board informed of everything I was doing and why I was doing it, all in the context of what it means to be the Church. I did not seek permission but understanding and acceptance. I think many on the Board were gratified to be able to support what they appreciated but were, for whatever reason, not able to do themselves.

Although I was technically appointed by the Bishop and Cabinet, the Board voted annually whether (or not) to request my reappointment. There were some "nays" each year, but an adequate majority of "yeas" always prevailed.

A Tribute to Charles Alston

This section on my sojourn in Milledgeville would be incomplete without an acknowledgement of my immeasurable indebtedness to Chaplain Charles Alston, my mentor, my inspiration, and my best friend on that journey.

I particularly recall our efforts to enlist other local clergy and church leaders in the work of Concern. Many were reluctant to become involved, fearing reprisals from others who opposed interracial activity. Charlie "explained" to me, as he often did, that these really were "good people." But that's not enough, he said. "You've gotta be good <u>for</u> something." Indeed!

Charlie had married into the black power structure. His wife, Constance Brown Alston, had an important position at the State Hospital. (Rose taught part-time in the program she directed.) She was a strong personality and a strong presence in any group. Equally important, though, her father was the long-time president of the local NAACP and a revered leader of the black community. The teacher who stirred the consciences of others to initiate the School Lunch program was her mother. Charlie had the connections to get things done.

Time after time, Charlie showed us how to stand up to the white power structure and insist that they "do the right thing." He understood all kinds of people and exuded tough love.

Over the years, in the midst of potential conflict, I've had a flashback to some earlier incident when Charlie was present, grateful for his example to guide me. Thank you, Charlie.

Part VII   Emory

Moving On

In late spring 1969, after the Board had already voted to request my reappointment for another year, my friend and colleague Lon Chesnutt, Methodist Campus Minister at Emory University, let me know he would be leaving to become pastor of an historically black church in the Georgetown area of Washington, DC. He suggested that I might want to consider applying for the position.

When I told Rose, she was immediately ready to go, even though she always hated moving. She had become increasingly uncomfortable living in a tiny apartment, having hardly any privacy, without any separation between work and home life, being available 24/7. She felt that our lifestyle was unfair to our sons. Moreover, she wanted to get a master's degree, and Emory, our alma mater, would offer that opportunity. We had both loved living in Atlanta and had a network of friends there.

There was one big problem, though. We both had fallen in love with Milledgeville, with the diverse community that embraced us there, and with the many opportunities each day to engage in work that "made a difference." To further complicate matters, I had already agreed to take the helm of Concern for the next year.

Nevertheless, we decided I should apply, just to see what the job might be like. When I interviewed with the Board, I learned immediately that my commitment to work ecumenically and my dedication to social justice were not "problems" but qualities they were seeking. When I met Dick Devor, the University Chaplain (a newly created position) who was leading an ecumenical team of ministers working collegially, I was convinced that Emory could be as fulfilling a place of ministry as Milledgeville had been. When offered the position, I immediately accepted, and the appointment system concurred.

After agreeing to purchase the home of Lon Chesnutt (my predecessor) in the Fernbank community just a mile from the Emory campus, we rented a U-Haul, filled it with our few possessions, and, holding back the tears, made our way to Atlanta. I can still visualize a group of students still around in the summer who had come over to help us move, standing on the front lawn of the Student Center waving goodbye, while Mrs. Koepps from next door swung on the dogwood tree by one arm, blowing us kisses.

Emory University, Again

For the second time in our marriage, we were moving in with Rose's parents. The home we had purchased from the Chesnutts had been rented until August, and our move was in late June. Also, for the second time, Rose's parents were in the process of selling their home at the time. As before, they welcomed us with open arms, this time with two kids as well. (You can see why I've never appreciated any of those nasty mother-in-law jokes.)

Although we were leaving a community where the ugly face of racism was visible all around us, we were not leaving racism, we soon learned. The family renting the house we had just purchased was black. While I think we knew that already, there was something else we did not know until new friends living up the street told us. The house had been vandalized by the teenage son of the neighbor next door as a protest against rental to a black family. Pink paint (the color of Pepto-Bismol) had been splashed across the front of the brick house. It had been completely cleaned (I think by the teenager himself), but we would occasionally find traces of paint on the lower limbs of some large boxwoods. Ours would have been identified as a "progressive" neighborhood, with many University families living there. We learned immediately that racism lived there as well. Apparently, only one black family lived in the area, but apparently one was too many.

In the fall, I joined the Executive Committee of the Druid Hills Fair Housing Committee. I can't recall any particular activity of that group, but I do recall that I learned a great deal about how housing discrimination operates to keep communities white.

Seminars on White Racism

As other colleges and universities in the South, Emory had traditionally barred black students. Even after the University of Georgia had been desegregated by court order (see above), Emory continued its tradition. The ostensible reason was that Georgia law still denied tax exemption to desegregated schools. Finally, a suit was brought by Emory and other schools challenging that law. A court ruling declared it unenforceable, of course, and Emory admitted its first black students in the fall of 1964.

By spring quarter 1968, there was finally a large enough black population to make their voices heard. Near the end of the term, activist black students had staged a protest in front of Cox Hall, the central dining facility, often frequented by people from the community, especially on Sundays. The protest had begun by interrupting the Sunday morning University Worship service underway nearby in the Theology Chapel. University Chaplain Dick Devor, who was leading the service, had wisely stepped aside and invited the protesters to voice their concerns. Following the service, they had moved on to Cox Hall, blocking the entrance.

University President Sandy Atwood had overreacted and sought an injunction in the local courts against the protests. Devor, who was a member of the President's "cabinet" (or whatever it was called), had argued unsuccessfully against the legal action. When he failed to stop it, he extracted a promise from the President that he would not use the incident at University Worship as a basis for the injunction. (I seem to remember that Georgia law made it a crime to interrupt a service of worship.) When the President failed to honor that promise, Devor had called him out publicly. (This is the version of events my campus ministry colleagues told me when I arrived. I suspect that the President would have described the incident differently.)

Charles Haynes, a remarkable freshman student, had been elected President of the student body that spring. Charles was, without a doubt, the most charismatic student I ever met. He was a devout follower of Meher Baba, an Indian spiritual master who, until his death earlier that year, had frequented a center in Myrtle Beach, South Carolina, where Charles and his mother, also a Baba follower, lived. When I first met Charles, it seemed there was an aura surrounding him. Although strikingly handsome, his magnetism transcended physical appearance. He spoke powerfully, but softly, with a gentle touch. He radiated goodness. I sometimes thought he was too good to be real, but the more I got to know him, I saw that he was all he appeared to be. Amazingly, he also knew how to rally large numbers of people to get good things done.

When students arrived in the fall, they were greeted with a multi-faceted, campus-wide program to combat racism. The centerpiece was a seven-week-long Seminar on Racism. Classes were organized for everybody at the University, students, faculty, and staff alike. A sophisticated study guide had been assembled. I was immediately enlisted to teach one of the dozens of classes.

All the groups on campus had been encouraged to incorporate the study of racism into our programs as well. United Campus Ministry (UCM, the collective of all the campus ministries) had planned a weekly seminar on "Black Theology and Black Power." Our Thursday luncheon discussions had been planned to include four sessions on racism.

UCM had also hired a part-time black staff member, Otis Turner, a graduate student in religion. (Otis would eventually become a part of the National Staff of the Presbyterian Church USA as Associate for Racial Justice.) Along with other ministries, Otis developed relationships with many of Emory's non-academic, low-wage employees, many of them black. After only one year, Emory eliminated funding for this position. (Does that sound like institutional racism?)

One of the programs I inherited from my predecessor was a Tutorial Project called SU-MEC operating out of two community centers in housing projects near the State Capitol. The student leaders had decided to postpone actual tutoring until January, utilizing the fall for learning about racism and equipping volunteers for working with kids who had been "left behind" in the school system.

Organized and led by the Student Government Association, in turn led by Charles, the campus-wide program forced the entire University community to deal with the racism tainting its life. For me, personally, the experience changed my life. Milledgeville had provided my experiential learning about racism in the flesh. The Emory program provided me with a more sophisticated understanding of the roots and current manifestations of racism in the culture. I think this may be the first time I heard the phrases "institutional" and "systemic" racism.

Koinonia Farm

In my first fall at Emory, a group of students and I spent a memorable weekend at Koinonia Farm near Plains. (See my earlier discussion of Koinonia's law suit against the Americus, Georgia, School Board above.) We were united in our desire to learn about living in intentional community. In the midst of rigid segregation patterns, Koinonia had maintained an interracial collective community for more than two decades.

We were there only months after the death of the community's founder, Clarence Jordan. On Sunday, the sermon was a recording of an earlier sermon by Clarence. It was almost as if he were still present. I wondered if the community could continue without his charismatic leadership. Surprisingly, it is still there today, having spawned Habitat for Humanity in the ensuing years. Although I was particularly curious to learn about how racism was dealt with in such a community, our visit was not long enough to get much insight into that issue.

Southeastern Campus Ministers Conferences

I have always valued highly collegial relationships with other campus ministers throughout the country and beyond, the more inclusive the better. In 1970 I was elected to the Executive Committee of the National Campus Ministry Association (NCMA) as the Southeastern Representative.

Near the same time, Clyde Robinson, part of the national campus ministry staff for the Presbyterian Church U.S., had been deployed as Southeastern Staff for United Ministries in Higher Education (UMHE), a vehicle for several mainline Protestant groups to do their work together. We decided immediately that it made sense for us to join hands in reaching out to our colleagues in the Southeast. In doing so, we became not only co-workers but good friends, a relationship that would continue for fifty years until Clyde's death in 2019.

The Southeast is different from other regions of the country. It has a stronger identity than geography, largely, I believe, because of the Confederacy. While ecumenical ministries were common in other regions, they were almost non-existent in the Southeast. Denominational campus ministers tended to be distrustful of "outsiders" (anybody from out-of-state), and that distrust was compounded when coupled with "ecumenical."

Nevertheless, with careful listening and response, we were able to sponsor the first Southeastern Campus Ministers Conference at the Atlanta Airport. It was well attended and enthusiastically received, and would be followed by others annually for ten more years, planned and carried out by a team selected at each conference. I want to tell you about one particular year, though.

The decision had been made to hold the Conference in the heart of Atlanta's black community, with lodging and meals at Paschal's. Conference attendees were always overwhelmingly white, and, for many, this was our first experience of immersion in a community where we were the minority. I recall the anxiety among the planners, myself included. Would we be safe? Would we be welcomed? Would anybody come? Of course, we were safe, welcomed, and many showed up to experience another "first" in their life's journey. As I recall the experience, though, I am keenly aware of the racism permeating our thinking and feeling.

A Sunday in April

After my first year at Emory, University Chaplain Dick Devor left for a sabbatical year in Houston, Texas. I agreed to fill that position for a year in his absence. At the end of his sabbatical year, he learned that his position, which had been funded by a three-year Danforth Foundation grant, would be terminated after one more year. Consequently, he decided to resign. I agreed to continue as the Acting University Chaplain for another year. (He believed, and I agree, that the elimination of his position was punishment for his calling out University

President Atwood for his failure to honor his commitment not to use interruption of University Worship as a basis for seeking the injunction against black student protests in the spring of 1969.)

In my second year in that role, while the General Conference of the United Methodist Church was meeting in Atlanta, I invited Theressa Hoover, General Secretary of the Women's Division of the Board of Global Ministries, to preach at University Worship. A lay woman, Ms. Hoover was the first African American to hold that position. Ms. Hoover preached a stirring sermon to an enthusiastic congregation.

After the service, I was standing in the large lobby outside the chapel. On a pedestal in the center of the area sits a bust of Bishop Warren Candler, after whom the school (Candler School of Theology) is named. I noticed Emory's retired Dean of Students, Hebe Rece, standing off to the side, chuckling. When I walked over to greet him, he told me why he was so amused. He was recollecting an occasion thirty-three years earlier when he had been in the same chapel on a Sunday morning.

In 1939, the Glenn Church congregation met there since its sanctuary had not yet been built. The preacher on that morning had been none other than Bishop Candler. He spoke passionately, Hebe said, about the upcoming General Conference that was to decide whether the Northern and Southern divisions of the Methodist Episcopal Church, separated in 1844 over slavery, would be reunited. He fiercely opposed reunion, Hebe remembered, and had warned the congregation, "If this Plan of Union passes, the next thing you know, there'll be a "N-word" standing in this pulpit." Hebe was enjoying the irony of the occasion and rejoicing that he had lived to see a preacher in the pulpit who was not only black but a woman as well.

I was reminded once more of how deep the roots of racism are buried in our church and society. I was also aware of how we continue to honor those roots in honoring such leaders.

(Incidentally, Bishop Candler was the brother of Asa Candler, founder of Coca-Cola, whose philanthropy enabled Emory to rise from its humble status as a small church college to its standing today as a world-class university. I learned, too, during the SGA Racism Seminars, about the partnership the two brothers formed to "Christianize" Cuba, allied with the oppressive government that was eventually overthrown by Castro.)

Summer Vocational Intern Program (SVIP)

The Summer Vocational Intern Program (SVIP), copied from a similar program in the South Georgia Conference created by Augusta Carruth, provided summer service opportunities for college students exploring careers in the church. I initiated the program for North Georgia probably in 1965. Increasingly over the years, we secured places for summer "internships" that were on the cutting edge of social justice ministry, usually in inner cities.

By the summer of 1970, we had incorporated the Georgia Conference (our still separate conference for black Methodist churches) into the program. It was probably that summer that Debbie Poole, an Emory student, applied and asked to be assigned to a program operating out of Trinity Church in the shadow of the State Capitol. (She had already been worshipping there most Sundays.)

Her parents did not just call; they showed up at my office, asking that I change Debbie's assignment to a "safer" neighborhood. As a parent myself, I could understand their desire to protect her from harm. However, I assured them that she would be working with a responsible agency. I made it clear that I deemed her a responsible young adult, and would her doing work she had a passion for. I agreed to change her assignment only if that was what she wanted. My recollection is that, in response to parental pressure, she decided not to accept the placement, but I may be wrong.

Again, I learned that an unreasonable fear of danger for whites in a black setting often controls our perceptions and our actions. Of course, I learned once more how difficult it is for parents to acknowledge the maturity of their young adult children. As an Emory medical school psychiatry professor, Jim Alford, tongue in cheek, told parents of first-year college students in a program we sponsored, "I Didn't Raise My Child To Be An Adult."

North Georgia Methodists for Church Renewal

By 1968 but perhaps sooner, a group of lay and clergy in the North Georgia Conference began to meet outside the regular church structures to "agitate" for structural change in the Methodist Church. We called our group North Georgia Methodists for Church Renewal. To my surprise, the most controversial subject we addressed was the Equalization of Clergy Salaries. I chaired our Committee on Racial Inclusiveness. (I thought that would be our most sensitive issue.)

The General Conference of the Church had already passed legislation mandating "negotiations" between the white conferences and the black conferences in each geographical area to develop a plan of merger. In Georgia, despite an episcopal leader of the white conferences verbally committed to merger, Bishop John Owen Smith, the process was painfully slow, with an abundance of "foot-dragging." Our "agitation" initially took the form of applying pressure to expedite the process.

Finally, a Plan of Merger was completed and presented for action. That segment of our Conference opposed to "race-mixing," demanding that we continue to maintain separate conferences and jurisdictions, immediately announced its opposition to the Plan (really, to any plan).

After closely examining the Plan, I and others were faced with a dilemma. The proposed Plan was clearly not a merger but an absorption of the black churches by the white conferences. Even the names of the "new" conferences were the same as the names of the previous white conferences. With separate conferences, the black conference had been selecting its own leaders and electing its own bishop. However, in the merged conferences, the overwhelming white majority would make those choices. Equally important, perhaps, was what I would term culture. The black conference had its distinct way of operating; the white conferences, another. The Plan did not address that difference at all; it simply assumed the white culture would predominate.

To clarify our thinking and assist us in determining our position on the Plan of Merger, several of us attended a meeting of Black Methodists for Church Renewal (BMCR), held in Savannah, as

I recall. We went to listen, not discuss. We were warmly received. At the end of the meeting, we were asked by BMCR to oppose the Plan. They opposed the Plan, we were told, not because they wanted to maintain separate conferences. Rather, their opposition, they made clear, was because the proposed Plan was unconscionable for the reasons mentioned above (and perhaps other reasons, as well). Those of us who participated in that gathering pledged our support. When the vote was taken at our annual conference, we voted against the Plan as they had requested.

This was perhaps the strangest moment of my activist life. I found myself voting with some of the most blatantly racist members of my conference, opposing some of the conference members I most respected. I found myself voting against legislation that would accomplish something I had vigorously advocated for years. Yet, how could I fail to support my black brothers and sisters when they were clearly being asked to forfeit their identity and their already-limited power?

Fifty years later, I think I did the right thing. At that moment in time, two ministers in the Georgia Conference were obvious leaders. One was Cornelius Henderson, whom I had first known in my youth when I was President of the Georgia United Christian Youth Movement, and he was Vice-President. He was a nice guy and worked well with white folks. The other was Joseph Lowery, who later became President of the Southern Christian Leadership Conference and a close colleague of Martin Luther King, Jr. After the merger, Cornelius Henderson rose quickly in the ranks and was eventually elected bishop. He never pushed a black agenda, never rocked the boat. Joseph

Lowery never again held a major leadership role in the United Methodist Church.

A Trip with Maurice Cherry

Sometime in the late 60s or early 70s, I had the good fortune to travel from Atlanta to St. Simons Island, Georgia, with Maurice Cherry. Maurice, a minister in the CME Church, was, at the time, Chaplain at Paine College, a historically black college in Augusta, Georgia. I had known him initially when we were both on the Board of the Georgia Council of Churches. On this occasion, though, we were traveling to Epworth by the Sea, as I remember it, for a meeting of the Georgia Commission on Higher Education. This was the first time I had driven through rural South Georgia in the company of an African American, and it became a memorable step in my education about racism. Of course, by this time, all public accommodations were theoretically open to people of all races. That was not the reality, though.

We weren't stopping overnight, fortunately. As we plunged deeper into the Deep South, I began to see the world around me through Maurice's eyes. We had to be attentive to bathroom breaks and places to eat. Everything I was accustomed to take for granted, Maurice had to weigh with great care. I don't recall any particular incident that occurred, but I do recall the feeling of always being on the alert for danger, just because he was black and I was white. That experience enabled me to catch a glimpse of what it must be like to be black in the South. (At the time, I had never heard of the Green Book, a guide for blacks needing accommodations in the South.)

The Anti-War and the Women's Movements

During my five years at Emory, both the Anti-War Movement and the Women's Movement dominated our lives. Four months after my arrival, I drove with five students to Washington, DC, for a protest march as part of the Vietnam Moratorium. I especially remember marching across the bridge from Arlington Cemetery, holding a candle and wearing the name of an American serviceman who had died in the War. Unfortunately, I had to return by plane the next day because the child of my best friend had died in Atlanta.

After the killing of four students at Kent State University by Ohio National Guard and two students at Jackson State University by Mississippi state troopers in the spring of 1970, I made the most difficult speech of my life—at a campus rally on the University Quad. Since this memoir is focused on racism, though, I will not write any more about this part of my life. I'm sure there were issues of racism permeating our national life, but they weren't central in my consciousness at the time. (My hurried research during this writing indicates that blacks were 14.1% of combat deaths, although only 11% of the country's population. A special program to recruit 100,000 soldiers in the late 60s netted 246,000 recruits; 41% of them were black.)

Special Addendum: Racism continues. In writing the above paragraph, I had, unintentionally, omitted the Jackson State University killings of black students from the subject of the campus rally. Why did I do that?

Rose was a tireless leader in the Women's Movement. My role (as hers had been throughout our marriage) was to be her supporter and cheerleader. I took on increased child care and meal preparation duties while she rallied hundreds of women to demand equal justice. She and Dana Greene (then a Ph.D. student at Emory, much later, Dean of the Oxford College of Emory) organized the most diverse group of religious leaders I've ever seen, the Atlanta Committee on Women and Religion. They met in our living room most of the time while I managed to keep the kids entertained elsewhere. She (along with Judy Leaming Elmer, later a member of the Secretariat of the Church's General Commission on the Status and Role of Women) created a grassroots United Methodist Women's Caucus that revolutionized the way the Church dealt with women. Rose has written about this extensively in her memoir (*A Passion for Justice*) so I will not repeat her story here.

The Barton Trust: Christopher Egwim

Ma Barton "found" Christopher Egwim through her vast network of friends. Elijah Moore, a United Methodist lay leader and a bank officer at Trust Company of Georgia in Atlanta, met Chris as a part-time worker at the bank and brought him to see her. Chris was an MBA student at Atlanta University, working at whatever job he could get to make ends meet. This is his story.

Born in a village near Onitsha in Southeastern Nigeria to a family of subsistence farmers, Christopher was trained as a teacher in Anglican mission schools. In his late 20s, he was able to go to Cuttington College in Liberia to study for his bachelor's degree. While there, a Civil War broke out back home. The world knew it as the Biafran War. When he completed his degree in 1967, the war was still raging, and he had lost touch with his family. People from his tribe, the

Christian Igbos, were being slaughtered by the more numerous Muslim Hausas, and many Biafran children were starving.

Unable to return home, Chris providentially found a sponsor, an Episcopal bishop in New York City, who arranged for him to come to Atlanta and provided a scholarship for his tuition. However, what Christopher needed most of all, in addition to supplemental financial assistance, was a family. That's where Ma stepped in. She embraced him with her all-encompassing love, and then she called us.

Chris soon became a beloved member of our family and would remain so until his death in 2005. To his widow, Winnie, his five children, Uchenna, Chuma, Jane, Chiedu, and Emeka, and his many grandchildren, I am still "Uncle Robert," appropriate since Chris was like a brother. This long-standing friendship has enriched my life in many ways. It has also enlarged my vision of racism. I'll share two stories to illustrate.

In the early 70s, while Chris was studying for his Ph.D. in Economics at the University of Georgia in Athens, he encountered what seemed like an insurmountable barrier. Although a superior student, Chris could not pass a required microeconomics course. The professor, a member of his Ph.D. committee, unapologetically declared, when Chris went to talk to him, that he did not believe black students were qualified to receive a Ph.D. degree.

A few months earlier, Chris had made friends with Dean Rusk, the former Secretary of State, when he had arrived to take a position at the University Law School. Chris, always resourceful, decided to enlist his help. When Dean Rusk heard his story, he simply said, "Let me take care of it." The microeconomics professor was soon removed from Chris's committee, and he easily completed his degree. Once more, the ugly face of blatant racism was exposed.

Sometime in 1971, Chris told me he thought he should get married since he was now into his 30s. Thus began my education about arranged marriages. (It was actually a continuation of my education. I had already learned much about the subject, as practiced in India, from Olivia Masih. See above.)

Chris had finally been in touch with his family in Nigeria. All had survived the War. Although conditions were still difficult back home, Chris said that his sister was willing to find a suitable marriage partner for him. Not being able to imagine such a system, I asked why he didn't consider seeking a relationship with someone here. He made it clear that he could, under no circumstances, marry an African American. When I asked why, he said, "Because almost all are descended from slaves." I made it clear that I considered his response to be racist in the same way as the attitude of the microeconomics professor.

Chris continued his correspondence with his sister, and, before long, she sent him a full description of Winnie Nwike, along with a photograph. Following his initial approval, weeks of correspondence began.

Chris would bring Winnie's letters for me to read, asking, "Do you think she is the right one for me to marry?" (He never showed me the letters he wrote to her in return.) After all the negotiations were complete, the marriage arrangement was made by appropriate representatives in Nigeria. Winnie boarded a plane for Atlanta, married to a man she had never seen.

Rose always said, "Winnie is the bravest woman I've ever known." During their next five years in this country, Winnie gave birth to three children and earned a master's degree in medical technology. After knowing them as a loving couple for the more than forty years of their marriage, I have learned to appreciate the custom of arranged marriage.

More Family Matters

When we moved to Atlanta in 1969, Mark entered the third grade at Fernbank School, an "elite" school in the DeKalb County system, directly across the street from the Fernbank Science Center. Bryan entered kindergarten at the Glenn Memorial Methodist Church Pre-school, a progressive program located on the Emory campus. Mark left the best teacher he ever had, Selma Erwin, and acquired the worst teacher he ever had. Both of Bryan's teachers were wives of men who had been my seminary professors—Mudie Weber and Gene May.

While both Bryan and Mark had been in minimally integrated classes in Milledgeville, their "sophisticated" Atlanta-area schools were all-white.

The Fernbank community was a wonderful neighborhood for kids. The backyard of our home bordered the back field of their school. They could safely ride their bikes all over the area, even to Emory Village. They were outside most days from morning to night, playing with a host of neighborhood friends. They were also involved in some kind of sports team each season through the local Y.

Friends at the corner of our block, Barbara and Wayne Langford, were their second parents, as we were for the Langfords' kids, Lori and Wayne. Bryan and Lori were best friends, while Mark claimed a set of best buddies, not all in the neighborhood.

Rose's main focus outside the home was her newly-found commitment to the Women's Movement. She also earned a Master of Arts in Teaching degree at Emory during our time there, as well as certification as a reading specialist—one course at a time. During our last year at Emory, she was a full-time eighth grade English teacher at Gordon High School, a formerly all black school in south DeKalb County.

As usual, I had no life other than family and a few close friends outside of my all-consuming job.

A Visit in Santa Fe with Sister Carmen

Since we lived on a single salary until 1973, and a small one at that, we had almost no money for family travel. I did receive, though, limited funds for continuing education. Using those funds, driving instead of flying, and carrying a big tent and pots and pans, we managed some wonderful adventures on our small budget. In the summer of 1970, I took two courses at Iliff School of Theology in Denver. We stayed in campus housing, and our sons literally had a ball—playing soccer from dawn to dusk with a group of boys their age, including the sons of Schubert Ogden, the visiting professor who was teaching one of my two classes.

On our circuitous route to Denver, we visited Santa Fe, New Mexico. A friend from our days in LaGrange had asked us to visit her sister in a Carmelite Monastery. Sister Carmen had been cloistered for almost twenty-five years, only leaving once for emergency surgery. We were making the family visit permitted annually, since no other family had been able to do so that year.

When we arrived, all four of us were ushered into the visitors' room, separated from the rest of the monastery by a metal barrier that could be seen through. There was something like a Lazy Susan that could be used for passing items back and forth. Although we had planned to pitch our tent at a nearby campsite, the nuns insisted that we bring our cots into the visitors' room and sleep there. They prepared our meals and passed them to us through the Lazy Susan. Rose observed that we were treated as if we were making a papal visit. Never before or since have I received such a hospitable welcome.

In that setting, we had two visits with Sister Carmen, whom we had, of course, never met. She exuded a kind of childlike innocence and was filled with questions, particularly about Atlanta and about Dr. Martin Luther King, Jr., whom she had only recently discovered was from Atlanta. Her lack of knowledge of the outside world was almost unimaginable.

Mark was nine that summer, and Bryan was six. She made a special effort to include both of them in our conversations. One particular conversation stands out. While we were discussing her life in the monastery, Bryan innocently asked the question all of us wanted to know but were too reticent to ask, "What do you do all day?" Sister Carmen immediately responded, "I pray."

Of course, that was not enough information for Bryan, who then asked, "What do you pray about?" Sister Carmen said, "I pray for racial justice." She then went on to tell us her story.

She had been a teacher in the segregated Atlanta public school system after World War II. She observed disturbing racial injustice firsthand and despaired that anything short of divine intervention could remedy the situation. So she had entered the monastery to pray for God to heal the racial divisions. All those years later, she was still doing just that.

After hearing Sister Carmen's testimony, I had a deeper understanding of what commitment to racial justice looks like.

Metropolitan Atlanta Higher Education Ministry (MAHEM)

Throughout my time at Emory, Emmett Herndon, the veteran Presbyterian Campus Minister, and I worked as a team. On a typical day, we might have coffee together in mid-morning and talk about some creative new idea for ministry. By the time I left for lunch, Emmett would probably hand me a one-page proposal for implementing it. It was an amazing working relationship, one I had never before experienced.

Both of us had become increasingly uncomfortable with the basic unfairness of how resources for campus ministry were allocated by our denominations among the Atlanta colleges and universities. The "whole pot" of money was being spent on Emory and Georgia Tech, while dozens of metropolitan institutions enrolling vastly more students were ignored. It looked elitist to us, since we seemed to be discriminating in favor of those schools where "our kind" studied. Except for a wonderful ministry by Episcopal Chaplain Warren Scott, the historically black institutions that were part of the Atlanta University System were not even on the churches' radar. We decided we would do something to try to change that.

We called our proposal <u>M</u>etropolitan <u>A</u>tlanta <u>H</u>igher <u>E</u>ducation <u>M</u>inistry (MAHEM). (The name may have been enough to seal its fate from the beginning.) We delineated a four-fold thrust, and proposed that the two of us be deployed part-time to launch the project. While our local ministry boards at Emory and the Presbyterian judicatory were willing to provide our services to launch this new work, the Methodist judicatory was not.

By this time, I had become so strongly committed to the project and was so "psyched up" for trying something new, that I could not simply file our proposal away. Providentially, I believe, at about the same time, I read a notice in the *Chronicle of Higher Education* announcing an opening for a campus minister to launch a metropolitan ministry in Jacksonville, Florida. It seemed strikingly similar to what we had proposed for Atlanta. So I applied, was called, and appointed.

Part VIII   Jacksonville

A New Start

As I re-read the sentence I just wrote, it sounds so simple, but leaving one place you love for another you've hardly even seen is never easy. I was excited about a new job and a huge creative challenge, on the one hand, but reluctant to leave the area that had always nurtured me and the family and network of friends from whom I drew my sustenance. Symbolically, all my life I had been called "Robert." In Jacksonville, when I introduced myself as "Robert," everyone would automatically convert that to "Bob." I didn't mind so much, but it was disorienting, causing me confusion about my real identity. In a way, it was like beginning my life over again.

On a hurried trip south earlier, we had bought a house (nicer than the one we were leaving) in a pleasant neighborhood near Jacksonville University. So we had a "nest" to settle into, but nobody around who "knew" us.

We arrived on the July 4th long holiday weekend. Our electrical power had not yet been turned on, and our belongings had not yet arrived. It was hot. Since Rose's parents were spending the week in Daytona Beach, fewer than two hours away, we retreated there.

Coming back the next day, a thunderstorm briefly but violently unleashed its fury on us. As it abated, we were treated to one of the most magnificent natural displays I have ever witnessed—two brilliant rainbows shining across the sky from one side of the horizon to another. We stopped the car to bask in their beauty, almost speechless with wonder and awe. My sagging spirits soared; my depression withdrew; and I began to feel "at home" again. (Rose always said that it took me about five minutes to feel "at home" in a new place, but it took her five years.)

Rose had not only left family and friends but a job she valued with no guarantees of a new one. Bryan, who would be entering fifth grade, seemed to take the move in stride, although his feelings are not always obvious. Mark was probably the most depressed of us all. He had just finished seventh grade and was extremely reluctant to leave his circle of friends. (He insisted, at one point, that he was not moving.) To make matters even worse, since he was attending pioneer camp at Camp Glisson the week of our move, we picked him up there for the drive to Jacksonville. He did not even have the chance to say "goodbye" to home. So he arrived awash in depression. Thank God for Jeanne Wallace, an "angel" his age in our new church. She refused to accept his reluctance to be social, took him under her wing, and insisted he participate in activities that slowly drew him out of his unhappiness. Rose's spirits lifted when she was hired to teach Reading at Southside Junior High School.

The Duval County School System had a peculiar desegregation plan. I don't recall all the details, but I am keenly aware of its impact on our family. In the fall, Mark began eighth grade at Ft. Caroline Junior High School, the first of two grades offered there. Bryan began fifth grade at Ft. Caroline Elementary School, the last grade offered there. Both schools were in our neighborhood, and, as I remember it, a few black kids were bussed there from across town. For our sons, there was very little impact that year.

The next year, though, Bryan was bussed way across town to a previously all-black school, Rufus Payne Sixth Grade Center. The daily bus ride was probably 45 minutes each way. His bus driver became a special person in his school experience. She would sometimes gather her riders on a weekend for a recreational experience. While I am grateful that Bryan had the experience of interracial education, I doubt that it was academically productive. I learned, though, to appreciate what black families had been enduring for decades when their kids were bussed past nearby white schools to attend black schools miles away.

The following year, Mark started 10th grade at Terry Parker High School in our neighborhood, where he would eventually graduate. For Bryan, though, it was another bussing year. He again had a long bus ride, although not as long as the previous year, to Douglas Anderson Seventh Grade Center just south of downtown. The year after, he was back in our neighborhood at Ft. Caroline Junior High School, then at Terry Parker High School. He spent grades 4-8 in five different schools.

We never considered private school. We probably could not have afforded it, but, more importantly, we were committed to public education. We believed that an important part of our kids' education was learning to understand, relate to, and appreciate people of different races, classes, and religions. Our sons have made different decisions about their kids, and we have not attempted to influence their decisions. We established an educational fund for each of our grandchildren at birth, adding to it each year on their birthday. We were thinking about college when we did so. When we were asked by our kids if they could use those funds for private elementary school, we left that decision to them. All of them have been educated almost exclusively in private schools. And, to quote Forrest Gump again, "that's all I have to say about that."

Jacksonville Campus Ministry

What was this spectacular ministry in Jacksonville that you were leaving all that was familiar to pursue, you might be wondering. It was the unique design of a group of folks from churches and colleges seeking to create what they had begun to call a "mutual ministry," to further the missions of both the colleges and the churches while respecting the integrity of each.

Ed Albright, Mission Developer for the Suwanee Presbytery, was the prime mover. (It was actually his D. Min. project for a degree from McCormick Theological Seminary.)

Although the vision included all the higher education institutions in Jacksonville and as many of the churches as could be recruited, it began with two colleges, Jacksonville University (JU) and the University of North Florida (UNF). Nine congregational partners and five denominational sponsors had pledged financial support. A very representative and active Board had been recruited and was at work, and an office had been arranged at JU. Our "program" was to be opportunistic, emerging out of an annual creative planning process involving our whole constituency. It did not yet exist; I was to become its "midwife."

Before I began to write this, I read all of the ten comprehensive annual reports from my tenure. I felt overwhelmed as I thought about how to capture those ten years in a few paragraphs. I functioned as a chaplain, especially at JU, and did a lot of praying at official events. I functioned as a pastor, and did a lot of marrying, memorializing, and leading worship (usually interfaith). I functioned as a counselor, and spent a lot of hours with individuals wrestling with important life decisions. I functioned as a preacher, occasionally on campus but more frequently supplying pulpits throughout Northeast Florida. I functioned as a teacher, especially at UNF and in local churches. (For example, I team-taught a popular UNF course, "The Meaning of Death," with other faculty a total of thirteen semesters.) I functioned as a communicator, writing columns for the student newspapers, the Florida Times-Union, and appearing on local TV and radio broadcasts.

Most significantly, though, I functioned as an enabler (in a good sense), helping a host of folks in the college and church communities identify and respond to opportunities for mutual ministries. Some examples of those included an annual Going to College Seminar for high school students; college courses team-taught by local pastors; International Student Host Family Programs; Resource Directories for both colleges and churches; seminars, study groups, lectures, workshops, film series on a variety of topics for church, campus, and community; Human Potential Seminars; Marriage Enrichment Weekends; Divorce Raps.

Edward Waters College

Although our vision encompassed all of Jacksonville higher education, our actual ministry began on only two campuses—as in Atlanta, those schools where "our kind" studied. Although I had come to Jacksonville, in part, because of a desire to remedy such racial bias, by 1980, we had yet to reach beyond our limited beginning.

Edward Waters College (EWC) was a 100-year-old, newly accredited, four-year liberal arts school across the river. Related to the African Methodist Episcopal (AME) Church, it had always been a second-class citizen in segregated Jacksonville. (Local leaders told me it would probably not survive another year. Then I learned they'd been saying the same thing for a hundred years.) Primarily because of the openness of Newton Williams, their Chaplain, EWC became a full participant alongside JU and UNF. Chaplain Williams and I agreed to be adjunct members of each other's ministry team, opening the door for new experiences for each of us.

I remember especially two occasions when several EWC students joined me at a Florida student conference in Leesburg sponsored by United Methodists. Usually an almost- if not all-white gathering, the experience was transformed by their presence.

Florida Junior College, Downtown Campus

The largest college in town, of course, was the local community college, enrolling more students than all the other schools combined. Florida Junior College (FJC) had multiple campuses, most of them across the river. The Downtown Campus had a 90% black enrollment, many of them non-traditional students.

Also in 1980, our ministry hired Granville Reed, a local AME pastor, to work part-time seeking to develop a ministry on the Downtown Campus and with black congregations. His diligent efforts had limited success on this campus where most students were present only for classes. After a year, our funding ceased as well.

I don't recall why we failed in this effort. I remember interesting conversations with the FJC President, a devout member of the Seventh Day Adventist Church. He never seemed to grasp our concept of mutual ministry, and, in the end, we were unable to formalize a relationship between the college and the ministry. We were unsuccessful, as well, in recruiting any black congregation to become one of our "participating" congregations, although one participated "provisionally" for a year. Several joined us in the Christmas International House program, though.

Christmas International House

Beginning in 1979, for two weeks of the Christmas break each year, we entertained 50 international students from all over the world studying in colleges and universities all over the country. We housed them in First Presbyterian Church downtown, sleeping on World War II surplus cots. Twenty-five or so churches and synagogues provided meals, trips, entertainment, family hosts for a day, transportation, and whatever else was needed to be good hosts.

This was our largest program annually, and impacted my life more profoundly than any other. I'll share just one story from the six years I coordinated this labor of love.

The finale event each year was an international smorgasbord prepared by our student visitors for all those who had been their hosts. The preparation was chaotic but, somehow, it always turned out to be a delightful evening. The highlight was always the entertainment provided by our student visitors.

The year was probably 1981. The evening before our finale, I had spent more than an hour with two groups of Chinese students trying to resolve a conflict. The first group was comprised of four males from the People's Republic of China. One of them seemed to be their leader; he was at least 6'6" tall. The other group was mostly female, all from Taiwan. Their leader seemed to be a very tiny but very forceful young woman. The two groups had been working all day on a presentation they were determined to do together, as one China. They had reached a snag, though. The Taiwanese group insisted that they include a folk song that the Mainland group objected to, claiming it had political overtones. Having exhausted my diplomatic skills, I finally gave up and went home, declaring, "You can just do your presentations separately." About 1:30 a.m., I was awakened from a sound sleep. The Chinese students were calling to say that, out of respect for their hosts, they had resolved their differences and would be presenting together.

Those six years provided much of my global education. I had not yet been out of the country (except for short trips across the Mexican and Canadian borders). However, each year, for two weeks, the world came to me and taught me about differences between people and cultures and how little those differences really matter in the end.

A Sermon at Arlington Presbyterian Church

Since I had no regular Sunday responsibilities, I was often asked to preach or teach in local congregations. More than any other church, I preached on several occasions at Arlington Presbyterian Church. Let me tell you about the last time. The scripture lesson was Mark 5:1-20. It's the story of the Gerasene demoniac healed by Jesus, culminating in the loss of a herd of swine. The climax of the story is that Jesus is asked to leave. I called the sermon "On Being Sane in an Insane World." It was rather direct about some of society's "insanities" that we have come to see as sane.

As I was greeting people at the door following the service, an older woman visiting on that Sunday gave me the highest compliment I've ever received. She told me, "That's the best sermon I've heard since I heard Harry Emerson Fosdick preach at Riverside Presbyterian Church in New York." I'm sure I beamed.

A few weeks later, the pastor told me that the Session, which must approve non-Presbyterian guest preachers, had voted not to invite me to preach there again.

I relate this story for several reasons. One is that I have said nothing in this memoir about preaching. That task is synonymous with the popular understanding of the profession. We even refer to its practitioners as "preachers." Although preaching has never been central for me as a campus minister, I have done a great deal of it.

Another reason is that I want to acknowledge the difficulty of what we ask pastors of churches to do every Sunday (or more often). We expect "preachers" to address a diverse congregation with opposing expectations and widely divergent views of the world and the church's role in it. How in God's name can they possibly "succeed?"

How many sermons have you heard about racism? If the answer is none, this reality might help to explain that.

Methodist Federation for Social Action

For more than a hundred years, the Methodist Federation for Social Action (MFSA) has been a force for social justice in the Church outside the regular structures. I have been a member for decades, certainly since the early 80s. More about this later.

One glaring social injustice within the Florida Conference of the Church, lamented by MFSA and the other campus ministries for years, was the omission of the only historically black state university in Florida, Florida A & M, from the Conference's funded ministries, although all other state universities were included. Whenever efforts were made to correct that injustice, they always failed "because no additional funds were available."

Around 1980, the black clergy caucus decided to take an extraordinary move to change that reality. When the conference budget was presented on the floor for adoption (usually a routine matter), one of the caucus members moved to amend the budget by adding, I think, $40,000 to fund a ministry at Florida A & M. (This is one of those things that "just isn't done.") They made their case, and, much to the surprise of us liberals who did not believe it could be done, the amendment was adopted.

I learned another lesson about combatting racism. It's perfectly acceptable to make folks feel guilty and then offer them a way to atone for their past. That lesson would have direct application for me later in another place.

Jacksonville Clergy for Alternatives to the Death Penalty

During my Jacksonville days, I was involved in numerous community groups. One was the Jacksonville Ministerial Association. There were black members; in fact, Navy Chaplain Carroll Chambliss, an African American, was President one year. However, most black ministers participated in a separate organization, the Jacksonville Ministerial Alliance. I remember working on a committee trying, unsuccessfully, to merge the two groups. I'm not sure I fully appreciated, at the time, why the separate organization was so important to the black clergy. I do now.

At one of our meetings, we had a presentation by a death penalty "abolitionist" I came to think of as the "angel of Death

Row." She had been fighting for years to gain access for visitors to the men on Death Row. Prior to that time, the only clergy allowed to visit were a group of fundamentalists whose goal was to "save the souls" of these men before they were appropriately executed. Having obtained a favorable court decision, she was asking us to sign up for a regular monthly visit to a section of Death Row. I signed up and began a journey unlike anything I'd previously experienced in my life.

Al Wells, pastor of First Presbyterian Church, and I volunteered for the same day each month and traveled to Raiford together. Each time we entered the prison, we began a lengthy process to reach the section we'd been assigned. There was a fence at least twenty feet high around the outside perimeter, topped by razor wire. I don't know how many electronic gates we passed through; they seemed to be interminable. The deeper we moved into the prison, the more foreboding it seemed. Finally, we reached the separate cell block reserved for those awaiting execution, and Al and I parted company to go to different sections. The cells in my section were side by side along a long hallway open on the opposite side.

I think there were fifteen or so inmates in my section, but I'll write about only three. One inmate was at least 65-years-old. He never seemed to be in touch with reality. He always wanted to talk about metaphysics, but I could never make sense of what he was saying. I remember learning later, after I had moved from Florida, that he had been executed.

Another was a young black man, under 25, from Jacksonville. I never chose to learn about anyone's crime. This young man, though, always wanted to talk about the charges against him, constantly insisting that he was innocent. I became convinced over the course of several months that he had indeed been wrongfully convicted. Had he not been young, poor, and black, he might have been able to afford adequate legal representation to establish his innocence. He had no family and was always crocheting afghans to sell for spending money. (I've always regretted not buying one from him.)

The third inmate on my block was in the last cell. Since he was from Jacksonville and had acquired considerable notoriety, I knew about his crime. He was convicted of abusing two of his children so severely that they died. I did not consciously make a decision to avoid him, but I never seemed to have enough visiting time to get all the way back to his cell. The other inmates, though, often talked about him; he seemed to be like a chaplain to the cell block. Apparently he had undergone a religious conversion and become a "new creation." I must confess that, when I finally forced myself to make the trip all the way back to his cell, I shared the positive view of the other inmates.

Al and I would discuss our visits on the way home. Al did most of the talking because one of the inmates on his cell block was the infamous Theodore (Ted) Bundy. Ted always had many stories to tell, some of them probably true.

My direct involvement with inmates on Death Row ended with my move from Jacksonville. However, I would never be the same. An inordinate percentage of the inmates on Death Row were, no surprise, black. It became clear to me that racism is the foremost reason for that excessive percentage. As I sought to coordinate this program of ministry to Death Row, it disturbed me that we were unable to enlist black clergy to make the monthly visits. I was never quite sure why that was true. One thing I knew to be true. Black clergy could have provided a much more meaningful presence for many black inmates than I and others like me were able to offer.

Part IX   Northern Virginia

Conferences and Consultations

I have always valued being a part of a network of co-laborers in the field of ministry in higher education. I've frequently taken advantage of opportunities to be with others pursuing the same goals as I. Because of the uniqueness of our ministry in Jacksonville, I was often invited to share what we were learning about ministry in the changing world of non-traditional students and institutions, about forging symbiotic relationships between colleges and churches, and about impacting the community outside the ivy-covered walls and stained-glass sanctuaries.

In May 1984, Rose had accompanied me to a national gathering of United Methodist campus ministers and chaplains in Baltimore, Maryland. While there, in a conversation with Jim McDonald, a colleague from Virginia, I learned about a job search underway by United College Ministries in Northern Virginia, an ecumenical ministry at Northern Virginia Community College (several campuses) and George Mason University, located in the Virginia suburbs of Washington, DC. I was immediately interested.

For ten years, I had been committed to staying in Jacksonville. Rose was in a job she loved as Director of the Academic Enrichment and Skills Center at UNF, and, for several years, had been pursuing an Ed.D. degree at the University of Florida while continuing to work full-time. And, of course, I didn't want to interrupt my sons' schooling.

As we drove through Northern Virginia on our way home, passing by exit signs for several of the campuses, I began to realize that Rose had completed her degree the year before. Mark was on his own, having decided to begin an MBA degree program at the University of Florida after a year teaching high school history and coaching sports in the Atlanta area following graduation from Emory. Bryan was at the University of Florida, too, completing his second undergraduate year. Maybe I was finally free to consider other vocational options. I also noted that I was about to turn 49, and an "old guy of 50" would find it increasingly difficult to be seriously considered for a higher education ministry job. This might be my last chance to do something different.

I loved doing ministry in Jacksonville, but I get bored easily. I had begun to feel I was repeating myself. I needed a new challenge. Northern Virginia would be an exciting place to live, I thought, and I would be able to create something new. I should mention that I already had a leg up on the job. I had been the major presenter at a conference in Richmond earlier that year, attended by some folks from Northern Virginia. And, too, Jim McDonald, who had told me about the job, was a member of the Board and a long-time friend. So I applied, was called, and appointed.

Our move to Alexandria was different from other moves. Our sons had left the nest. Again, though, Rose was sacrificing a job she loved, unsure of another. Again, we were starting over, unacquainted with the place or the people. I found that newness exciting; Rose found it depressing. The job she found, teaching six classes of junior high school Chapter I remedial reading classes, was, as she described it in her memoir, "a new challenge every three minutes." She called it her "hardest year of teaching."

We were not able to sell our house in Jacksonville for a year, and were still funding college and graduate school expenses of our sons. To compound the financial pressures, we had moved to an area where real estate prices were almost double those in Jacksonville. A "bridge" loan for a year from my parents, though, enabled us to purchase a three-level townhouse outside the Beltway, between Springfield Mall and Ft. Belvoir. We found a "church home" at Mt. Vernon United Methodist Church, near "that" Mt. Vernon, and the pastor and his spouse soon became our best friends.

United College Ministries in Northern Virginia

United College Ministries in Northern Virginia (UCMNV) had been struggling to do ministry in the Virginia suburbs of DC for eighteen years, never with more than a part-time staff. Its father figure was Dan Shumate, a retired CIA career officer (I always thought he had been a "spook," though he would not confirm or deny it). He was now adjunct faculty at George Mason University and active in a nearby Methodist church. He was the dreamer who persevered over all those years to assure that the Church would not abandon this new arena of higher education, so different from the residential colleges of the past.

Among others, three clergy were leading this most recent effort to "do a new thing." They were two Episcopal priests (Richard

Corkran and John Clyde Millen) and a United Methodist pastor (Emmett Cocke).

George Mason University was a new "star" in Virginia's University System. Since its founding soon after World War II, it had been expanding exponentially. Its students were still largely commuters, of course.

Northern Virginia Community College was a "star" in the national community college movement. Established in the 60s, it was the largest higher education institution in the state. Its students were from almost every country in the world. Our ministry sought to have a presence on five of its campuses spread throughout the metropolitan area in Virginia—Alexandria, Annandale, Loudoun, Woodbridge, and Manassas.

We began with a single staff person—me. St. James United Methodist Church, across from the Alexandria campus, generously provided an office for our use. We contracted with their secretary for a few hours of office assistance weekly. The first fall we had two part-time chaplains, one at George Mason and one at the Annandale campus, both Wesley Theological Seminary students fulfilling field education requirements.

Multiracial, Multicultural Staffing

One of the unique challenges we faced was the multi-ethnic, multi-racial, multi-faith, multi-national, multi-everything character of the student bodies. Not only did we view this as a challenge; we saw it as a gift as well. Early on, we determined that we must find ways to connect to that reality.

Metro Washington had unique resources for ministry. It is home for several theological schools and underemployed clergy. We devised a plan to link those resources to that multi-everything reality by employing part-time chaplains to serve particular campuses and/or particular racial/ethnic populations. Our chaplains were usually seminary interns earning field education credit; other times, they were underemployed local clergy, doing our ministry along with another.

During my thirteen years at UCMNV, we employed thirty-seven different campus chaplains. We learned that the best way to demonstrate that we were serious about ministry with a variety of racial ethnic groups was to reflect diversity in our staff. Half of our chaplains during those years were persons of color—from four different racial ethnic groups. In the latter years, we often had four chaplains, each from a different racial ethnic background.

Trying to "supervise" this diverse staff was one of the most productive learning experiences of my life. I learned to see communication in a whole new way. I remember one Korean chaplain whose English language skills were limited. I might ask if we could meet on a particular day at a particular time. He would say "yes," but not appear at the appointed hour. When asked why he had failed to show up, he would say that he did not know we were meeting. I learned that when he said "yes" to my question, he was indicating only that he understood what I had said. He was not understanding that he had agreed to meet me then. I learned that communication is more than what one says or intends to say. It is what is heard by the recipient of the speech.

I learned to value customs, foods, traditions, theologies, ways of being that I had never before encountered. I learned as well that my customs, foods, traditions, theology, and ways of being are not superior as I had always assumed them to be.

I learned to appreciate the courage of a black female chaplain willing to walk bravely into a gathering of the Muslim Student Association knowing that women are not generally welcomed there. I learned to empathize with the Korean chaplain living at home in a multi-generational family seeking to navigate between the worlds of his grandmother, unable to speak English, and his Korean American peers, unable to speak Korean. I learned to appreciate the young African American chaplain's struggle to reconcile what he was learning in seminary with his fundamentalist church experience.

I was often amazed at our success in getting funding to support these chaplains from denominations struggling to make ends meet. I think I know why. The churches sincerely wanted to enlarge their outreach to non-white groups. The problem was they had no idea how to do that. These mostly young neophyte ministers were offering them a way.

Apartheid in South Africa

If you are an activist, Metro Washington is a wonderful place to live. Although I am an infrequent protest marcher, when I learned about the series of daily protests being organized in front of the South African Embassy, I knew I wanted to be a part of this witness against apartheid.

Rose and I both showed up on our appointed day. There was a large crowd, maybe because Peter, Paul, and Mary were participating that day. The protest was well orchestrated. Arrests were made, not of everyone marching but of a select few, including our celebrities of the day. It was extremely civil. After those arrested were loaded into the paddy wagon and transported to jail, those of us left behind went home to a nice dinner.

Did our presence make a difference, I wondered. Maybe so, like a handful of sand poured into a sandbag, in turn added to a levee to stop a flood. Primarily, though, I know it made a difference in my life. It made the reality of apartheid come alive to me. It strengthened my commitment to do something about my complicity, indirectly, through investments. No big thing, but something.

Virginia Campus Ministry Forum

In 1988, I added a new responsibility—Coordinator of the Virginia Campus Ministry Forum. Loosely related to the Virginia Council of Churches, this organization is, as the name suggests, an arena for conversation about campus ministry. It is broadly ecumenical, even including Roman Catholics and Southern Baptists. Since I've been an "ecumaniac" most of my life, I was pleased to fill this role. Because the Forum and its coordinator had played a key role in resourcing the Northern Virginia ministry, my Board enthusiastically supported this arrangement.

I visited most of the campuses in Virginia where the church was at work. My awareness of the scope of our ministries and the unmet challenges still awaiting us grew enormously during my nine years in this role. The culminating event for me was leading a state-wide Conference on Re-Imaging Ministry on Campus just before my retirement.

More Family Matters

Fortunately, after three years in Northern Virginia, Rose was able to move to a different job in the Alexandria School System that she came to love—Reading Resource Teacher at Hammond Junior High School. About a year later, we moved into the school neighborhood, only four or five blocks from her school and about two miles from my office. (Since I'm writing about racism, it should be noted that our house was on Pegram Street, named for Confederate General John Pegram.)

To make our move even more wonderful, we were in the parish of Fairlington United Methodist Church, a progressive congregation where our friends Emmett and Lucy Cocke had moved a year earlier.

Rose had begun work a year or so earlier on an historical novel she was tentatively calling *The Salzburgers*. The story of some of the earliest settlers of Georgia, her cast of characters included some of her own ancestors. She soon formed a writing group of women with whom she would share her creations (and her life) for the rest of her days. In 1988 and again in 1990, we made our first overseas trips, focused on visits to Salzburg, Austria, and environs, the setting for much of her story.

Meanwhile, our sons were composing their own lives apart from us, as is appropriate. After living together for two years at the University of Florida, they had become adult friends rather than two kids wrestling on the floor for dominance.

Bryan graduated first, in December 1985, found a job in human resources in Jacksonville, bought a condominium, and settled in. He found Laura Neal, a Jacksonville native, working in a mortgage company there and soon determined that she was the one for him. They were married in 1988 at the Jacksonville University chapel, with me as officiant and Mark as best man. Within the year, Bryan's company transferred him to Dallas, Texas, where they began their 28-year sojourn as Texans. Laura took a new job with Arrow Industries and began work toward her undergraduate degree, while Bryan enrolled in an MBA program after hours.

Mark completed his MBA in May 1986, moved back to Atlanta, and took a job in the management training program of a bank. It took him longer to find the one for him. At his tenth high school reunion, though, he met Jill Saul, a member of his huge graduating class at Terry Parker High School but not among his acquaintances. Jill was (and still is) a flight attendant with American Airlines. They were married in 1990 at the Glenn Memorial Chapel on the Emory campus, with me as officiant and Bryan as best man. In fewer than two years, they had moved to Dallas, too, just two blocks from Bryan and Laura.

One other family member was added during this period. In a picnic basket with a red bow at Christmas 1988, Bryan and Laura presented us with a puppy. We named him Teddy, since he looked like a teddy bear. We had not known we wanted another dog, but he came to light up our lives for the next fifteen years.

Betty Williams (Perkins)

Betty Williams (Perkins) shared the 1976 Nobel Peace Prize with Mairead Corrigan as a founder of the Peace People in Northern Ireland. They had mobilized tens of thousands of people to demand an end to the sectarian violence in Northern Ireland known as the Troubles.

I became acquainted with Betty while I was living in Jacksonville. She was an inspiring speaker and a dynamic witness to the power of committed activists to end violence. In both Jacksonville and Northern Virginia, we sponsored Betty in a series of presentations on "Ordinary People Can Change the World." With a broad coalition of colleges and churches as co-sponsors, events on all our campuses and in selected churches reached hundreds of persons with her motivating message. It was probably our most "successful" of all programs, if you judge by numbers.

The story I want to tell, though, is something that happened on the morning Betty spent with Rose's class of diverse junior high students, many of them immigrants. Rose had been reluctant to ask Betty to come to her school to meet with her small classes of special students. I encouraged her to do so, believing that it would be a good experience for both Betty and the students. When she approached Betty about it, she enthusiastically agreed.

Betty often spoke about her visit with Joan Baez to a refugee camp in Laos after the Vietnam War was over. Conditions there were desperate; children were literally dying before they could be removed by the relief agency. After she related her experience, a shy Cambodian pre-teen approached her and began to share his story. He and his brother had been in such a camp after literally fleeing for their lives from the Khmer Rouge. She tearfully embraced him, offering him a level of understanding and acceptance he had probably never before experienced. It was a magical moment I'll never forget.

An Evening with Toni Morrison

When I learned that Toni Morrison was scheduled to speak at George Mason University, I knew that I wanted to be present. I'd read her books and knew her to be a gifted writer and storyteller. I was disappointed, upon arrival at the lecture, to learn that she was simply going to read the first few pages of her new novel, *Beloved*, as yet incomplete.

When she began to read, though, my disappointment became delight. I was mesmerized, hanging on every word. I can't recall ever having a more enchanting evening, before or since. I'd never heard the English language spoken more eloquently or used more effectively.

I recently watched a conversation with Ms. Morrison on PBS's American Masters. (I wondered if anyone else felt discomfort because of the name of that series, especially when Toni Morrison is the subject.) Since I've been so focused on racism while writing this, I immediately remembered that night and began to examine my reaction. Granted, her use of the English language is miraculous. After all, she is a Nobel Prize winner. But I think my unconscious racism was at play as well. I have been so conditioned to think of African Americans as "less than" whites that such linguistic brilliance by a black person still amazes me in a way that it would not if that person were white. I am thankful that this writing is clarifying my life experience and helping me see what, heretofore, has been hidden from me.

Victoria Gray Adams

Victoria Gray Adams was one of my campus ministry colleagues in Virginia. However, she was far more than that. She, along with Fannie Lou Hamer and Annie Devine, was a founder of the Mississippi Freedom Democratic Party, challenging white rule at the 1964 Democratic National Convention. Backed by her party, she unsuccessfully challenged longtime Mississippi Senator John Stennis in that year's senatorial race.

When I knew her, though, she was a Methodist laywoman living in Petersburg, Virginia, determined that her denomination would have a presence on the local college campus, Virginia State College, one of Virginia's two historically black state schools. Since nobody else seemed to be willing, she became the volunteer, part-time campus minister.

The United Methodist Church in Virginia, like the other two states where I had lived, had established ministries on almost all the state college and university campuses except the historically black ones. Campus ministers had been trying for years to correct that inequity. We had finally secured funding for ministry at Norfolk State University through normative channels, but our efforts to include Virginia State had failed.

I remember a conversation with Vicky at that time. We talked about strategy; she wanted to know what I knew about how other historically black schools had accomplished what we had been unable to do. I told her about the successful effort by the black ministers' caucus in Florida, but no further action was taken at that time.

Early in 1997, after I had announced my plan to retire that summer, Vicky called me. She said she was ready to act and asked if I would help her. She contacted Virginia's black ministers' caucus, and they agreed to offer a motion on the floor of the conference to amend the budget to include funding for a full-time ministry at Virginia State. I wrote the appropriate motion, and Vicky took it from there. I carefully prepared a speech to support the proposal, reciting my experience in both Georgia and Florida where similar inequities had existed, asking, "Is it not time to do the right thing?"

When the motion was made to adopt the conference budget, Alton Washington, a respected black clergy leader, rose and made his motion to amend. It was wholly unexpected, out of the ordinary, and ignited a flurry of speeches questioning the appropriateness of the proposed action. The Conference Council Director, the Chair of the Council on Finance and Administration, and others insisted that "this is just not the way we do things." However, the motion was clearly in order, and the Bishop ruled that the debate could proceed.

The first speaker, as I recall, was a white youth delegate from a small church. He spoke from the heart and from his own experience about how this was clearly the right thing to do. Then an elderly white woman from a rural community, soft spoken but her voice charged with controlled emotion, shared her journey to racial inclusiveness. That alone did it. I spoke, too, but what I said was anticlimactic after the power of these two speeches. When the vote was taken, probably 90% voted for our amendment.

This was my final annual conference session. Many times throughout my career, I had advocated unsuccessfully for lost causes. At last, a longstanding wrong had been righted. I felt that I had been given a retirement gift.

Building Our Dream House

In the summer of 1992, we had spent a week, as was our custom, at the condominium in Daytona Beach, Florida, which had been purchased originally by Rose's parents, then sold to Rose's sister Mary. We were already looking ahead to retirement, and Rose suggested we return north driving on the beachfront, looking at properties along the way. We did, all the way to Beaufort, South Carolina. We saw one beachfront lot that we immediately fell in love with—in a new development in Flagler County (halfway between St. Augustine and Daytona Beach) called Hammock Beach Estates. It was the southeast corner lot just behind the dunes, with county parkland in front and to the south. It would provide panoramic views of the ocean and beachfront, as well as uncultivated ocean scrub. There was one problem. Until we sold our house in Virginia, we would not have the money to buy it.

The following summer, following our annual vacation in Daytona Beach, we again drove by to see if the lot was still available. It was, but we still had the same problem. During an ice storm in Virginia the following winter, we had a call from the developer offering us a "deal." He was willing to reduce the price by $25,000. We began to think more seriously about how we might arrange to buy it before retirement.

By this time, we thought we could afford to retire in 1997, the summer I turned 62. Rose would be 60. The solution we discovered was to refinance our house in Alexandria (with a mortgage at a low, adjustable rate for five years). We could then use our equity to purchase the lot in Florida. That's what we did—in 1994.

Then in late 1995, the developer called us again with another "deal." He would build our house now and lease it back for a year to show as a model, paying us a monthly rental equal to our mortgage payments. That looked like a good plan to us, and we said "yes." Our "dream house" was completed in 1996. When we visited it that summer, we could hardly wait to move in the following summer.

More Family Matters

There were several reasons driving our 60s retirement decision. While we still loved our jobs, they were both demanding. We had little time for anything else, and we had other agendas for our remaining years.

Our family was both expanding and contracting, and we wanted to have more available time to devote to their care. Our first granddaughter, Samantha Paige Thomason, was born on May 7, 1993, to Mark and Jill in Dallas. Later that year, Rose's mother, Mary Bennett Shearouse, died at Magnolia Manor, a retirement community in Americus, Georgia, while Rose was enroute to be present at her death.

Mark and Jill moved to Ft. Lauderdale, Florida, near Jill's mother and stepfather, not long before our second granddaughter, Callie Elizabeth Thomason, was born on December 8, 1995.

My father, Albert Troy Thomason, had been in declining health for years after a series of small strokes. When he could no longer be cared for at home, he moved to a nursing home for his final months, where my mother visited each day. He died in Dalton on January 1, 1996. I was able to be at his bedside.

Bryan and Laura's first daughter, Alaina Mae Thomason, was born in Dallas on August 1, 1996.

We wanted to be available to assist in the care of our remaining parents and my sister Helen, severely handicapped since birth. We also wanted to be a part of the lives of our grandchildren (and others to come) in Dallas and Ft. Lauderdale.

Rose wanted time to write, and she did. My ambition was to be a beach bum, a lifestyle I utterly failed at, although I did learn to enjoy a long walk on the beach every morning at sunrise.

Christopher Egwim arrived from Nigeria for a month as we began packing for our big move. He hoped to find a college and scholarship for his only son born in Nigeria, Chiedu, but we were not able to accomplish that. However, he was able to be a part of the wonderful sendoff we were given by the ministry and the school system in Northern Virginia. Mark, Bryan, Laura, and Alaina joined us for the big production hosted by the UCMNV Board.

Part X   The Retirement Years

The Big "C"

Rose had been concerned for several weeks about what she perceived as "not right" about her right breast. Mammograms and needle biopsies had not revealed the problem, but she had insisted on another biopsy during our last week in Northern Virginia. She had not been able to get the result of the test before we started our journey to Florida. However, she was assured she could talk to her doctor the next day at Noon. She suspected trouble.

The next day, she called from a very hot phone booth somewhere in North Carolina to learn that the result was "very suspicious" and that she should see an oncology surgeon right away. Although we had left all our doctors behind, she was able to make an immediate appointment with a wonderful doctor at Mayo Clinic in Jacksonville. Less than two weeks after our arrival in Florida, she had a mastectomy, followed by chemotherapy and radiation treatments. She has written extensively about that in her book, *Shoring Up My Soul: A Year with Cancer*, so I shall not repeat the story here. I will simply say that I learned a new way of being a caregiver that challenged but enriched my life.

The year 1997 could hardly have been a more eventful year for us. In addition to dealing with Rose's cancer, on November 11, our first (and only) grandson, Troy Neal Thomason, was born in Dallas. On Thanksgiving Day (November 27), after a traditional dinner in his villa with daughter Betty and some of her family, Rose's father, Herbert Samuel Shearouse, still living at

Magnolia Manor in Americus, died suddenly. It felt like 1993 all over, gaining a grandchild and losing a parent. Rose coped, as always, by writing a poem about the experience.

By summer, though, following a year of debilitating treatments, it appeared that Rose's cancer had been eradicated. We celebrated by joining old friends from Jacksonville, John and Joanne Wallace, on a three-week tour and cruise to Alaska.

After taking a break of about a year to process her experience, Rose wrote her memoir *Shoring Up My Soul: A Year with Cancer*. We published it during her final year. It was a therapeutic experience and has been a gift to many who have read it.

National Campus Ministry Association (NCMA)

NCMA, the professional association of campus ministers established in 1964, had been an important part of my life beginning in 1966, my first year in Milledgeville. I had served a three-year term on its Executive Committee, been Coordinator of its Partnership Program, helped plan several of its summer conferences, and attended almost all of them. The network of colleagues all over the country related to NCMA had been my lifeline throughout the 31 years I had labored on campuses.

I had known that George and Sally Gunn, longtime friends who were handling staff responsibilities for the organization, had planned to retire from their roles at the end of the year. I offered myself as their replacement, and was soon hired. It was the perfect retirement job. I received a small stipend, but, as I have often said, I would have done the work gratis.

I edited the quarterly newsletter, provided the membership services, published "Occasional Papers," met with the Coordinating Committee, and sometimes handled summer conference registration. During the nine years I was in the position, it acquired a new and more descriptive title, Administrative Officer. I loved the work, the many opportunities to be creative and learn new skills, the nurturing relationships, and the freedom to do most of my job on my own time schedule from my home office attired in a swimsuit and flip flops.

Palm Coast United Methodist Church

When we retired to Palm Coast, at a time we most needed a caring church community, we did not have a church home. Of course, we had what I've now learned to call a virtual community, supporting us from many places. And we had Rose's "designated minister," Martha Rutland, a longtime friend, then working as a hospice chaplain in DeLand, Florida, not too far distant.

We lived miles away from "civilization." It was at least seven miles across a toll bridge to the nearest grocery store. We had visited all the United Methodist churches within twenty miles of our house. Only one bothered to respond to the visitor's card we left in the offering plate. None felt compatible; they certainly did not feel like the warm community at Fairlington we had left behind.

Eventually, we "hung our hats" at Palm Coast United Methodist Church. The best part of the experience is that we found our new best friends there, Elwyn and Ann Williams. Elwyn was a retired minister who had worked in development on college campuses in Ohio, Oregon, and Florida. Ann, like Rose, was a breast cancer survivor.

The Palm Coast Church was multi-racial, a feature that made it especially attractive to us. Maybe 20% of the members were non-white, and, even more importantly, several of the lay leaders were non-white as well. Most were Jamaicans who, as we soon learned, had grown up with different traditions than most of the African Americans we had known. Although she never liked women's circles, Rose joined one that was mostly Jamaican women. At some point in each meeting, they would serve what was clearly "high tea." She loved the experience and the women who welcomed her so warmly.

The dominant theology in the congregation was fundamentalist. We visited every Sunday school class, but, whenever I would say something in response to a fundamentalist position, it would be met with puzzlement, as if I were speaking in a foreign language. There was no pushback. Folks were always polite, but would simply ignore what I had said and move on with "the lesson." Rose and I soon quit saying anything (easier for her to do than for me) and just quit going.

The pastor spent much of the time in the very informal service making everybody feel welcome. Some Sundays there was a scripture reading; some Sundays, not. There was very little liturgy, and the music (both electronic organ and piano) was gospel swing. The sermon was an updated version of Norman Vincent Peale. There was a great deal of friendliness, but it felt superficial. There was virtually no visible mission outreach.

About the only place of service I found was to serve communion to shut-ins, a ministry organized by a delightful woman from "the islands." The pastor apparently was not available for this service but was happy for me to provide it.

Heavenly Hospitality

When you live in Florida, especially if you're on the beach, and you know folks "up North," expect a steady stream of visitors, make that a flood in the winter. I loved having visitors, and so did Rose, even though she was much more introverted than I. She was the one who talked about "heavenly" hospitality. Because we had lived in several places, we learned early on the lesson of the camp song, "Make New Friends, but Keep the Old. One is Silver and the Other, Gold."

We had visitors from all over the country, even some from other countries. They brought us many gifts with their tales of adventures and deep sharing about their life journeys. We loved having our grandchildren visit, especially when we had them to ourselves without parental restraints. (We enjoyed our kids, too.)

The only time Rose said, "I'm not going to do that again," was when we hosted the NCMA Coordinating Committee of maybe ten campus ministers for three or four days. Later, after her death, I tried it again. Then I, too, said, "I'm not going to do that again."

More Family Matters

A very big event happened in our lives on June 15, 1999. Our triplet granddaughters, Jessica Marie, Julia Kate, and Rebecca Jane were born to Bryan and Laura in Dallas. Our cup overflowed. We were there for their birth, having "moved in" five weeks earlier to help care for Alaina and Troy while, even though she struggled to do so, Laura successfully carried them to term.

In the spring of 2000, we received the life-shattering news that Rose's cancer had metastasized. She had been to see her St. Augustine oncologist, Danielle Montgomery, for a routine check-up. Following the visit, Dr. Montgomery's nurse called to say that she needed to come in to discuss the results with Dr. Montgomery. That sounded ominous.

Although we had planned to leave that day to attend Grandparents' Day at our granddaughters' school in Ft. Lauderdale, we agreed to come in for an afternoon appointment. When we were seated in her office, Dr. Montgomery shared the bad news. The cancer had spread to the liver and spleen. She showed us the pictures and explained how pervasive it was.

Rose was always prepared for the worst. Since she already knew that metastatic breast cancer is not curable, she wanted to know about treatments and prognosis. Dr. Montgomery assured us there were chemotherapies available that could slow the spread and recommended a course of treatment. Rose's first question was, "How long do I have?" Dr. Montgomery replied, "Maybe three years." We both appreciated her candor, accompanied by a level of empathetic care never witnessed before or since.

When we left her office, we made the decision to go ahead with our plan to drive to Ft. Lauderdale, knowing it might be the last Grandparents' Day Rose could attend. We decided at that moment that we would live whatever time left to us with as much gusto as possible. We also decided to be transparent throughout the experience, sharing what was going on with all those we loved (a large circle), and accepting their participation in the journey when offered.

Rose lived a little more than a year after that, dying on Palm Sunday, April 8, 2001, with Mark, Bryan, and Laura with me at her bedside. (Jill was caring for the grandchildren.) During her final year, she was able to do three things particularly important to her. On April 11, 2000, she joined her longtime friend Nancy Grissom Self to make a speech to women students at Candler School of Theology, Emory University, describing their pioneering work in the Women's Movement in the United Methodist Church. (*A Passion for Justice*, pp. 115-123)

Later that spring, she attended her first high school reunion, celebrating the 45th anniversary of her graduation from Avondale High School and reconnecting with friends she hadn't seen since commencement. And throughout her final year, she wrote the stories of her life, primarily for our seven grandchildren.

We celebrated her life at three events. At Palm Coast United Methodist Church on April 11, Martha Rutland (her "designated" minister) and Bishop Charlene Kammerer officiated. Martha also went with Mark, Bryan, and me to officiate at the graveside when we buried her cremains in the Thomason Family plot in West Hill Cemetery in Dalton on April 14. Her Alexandria writing group facilitated a service later in April at Fairlington United Methodist Church in Alexandria, led by three women clergy. Mark and Bryan created a short clip from the video of her Emory speech, which was played at two of the services. Bryan wrote a song which he sang at all three services, leaving everyone in tears. (*A Passion for Justice*, pp. 133-134)

Joy in the Morning

How do you survive when the light goes out of your life? Rose had been at the center of who I was and what I wanted to be and do for all of my adult life. I hardly knew what to make of life without her. As those of you who know me well would expect, I coped with my huge loss as I've lived my life for as long as I can remember; I immersed myself in as many meaningful activities as I could manage.

When Rose died, she was on the Board of our local chapter of the American Cancer Society. She had been scheduled to participate in the annual Relay for Life in just two weeks. The Board wanted to dedicate the event to her, and asked if I would offer an invocation at the opening. Somehow I did, though I wondered if I would be able to speak. I learned from that experience and many more to follow that, for me, plowing ahead through all the emotionally difficult moments is the path to healing. Each one hurt, but not as much as the one before.

I especially remember an occasion in September of that year when Rose's Aunt Nina Fetzer died. Nina's daughter, Mary Dean, asked if I would officiate at a graveside service in Pooler, Georgia. Of course, I said "yes." When we were all gathered at the gravesite, though, and I opened my mouth to speak, no words emerged. I was about to panic, but I somehow regained my composure and proceeded with the service as I had done many times before in my life. Until that moment, I had not realized how raw my emotions still were and how far I had to go before I was whole again.

Slowly, one painful episode after another, I discovered the truth that I had often quoted to others: "Weeping lingers for the night, but joy comes with the morning." (Psalm 30:5)

Publications

When Rose died, she had been seeking a publisher for her historical novel. While I was not up to the task of seeking an agent and publisher, I decided to publish and market it on my own.

My first task was to make decisions about the final text, including title. Rose always wrote in the context of a writing group. Although she had left her Alexandria group behind, she had formed another in Palm Coast. She had been sharing her novel with them, chapter by chapter, writing down their suggestions for revisions. I first had to decide whether she was just noting a suggestion or making a change in the manuscript.

Then there was the title. She had been toying with the idea of calling her book *The Grandmother Trees*, even rewriting the first few pages to reflect that title. Had she made the decision to do so? With the invaluable help of Lorraine Ruhl, one of the group, I made all those decisions and published the book in the final days of 2001.

However, I was not finished. When she died, Rose was writing a memoir for our seven grandchildren "so that they might know the strings that connect the generations." She had written eighteen vignettes and was still at work when time ran out. In 2010, I decided to publish those along with other writings by both of us. I called it *A Passion for Justice: Memoir of a Shared Life*. I included in it selected newspaper articles I had written over ten years for a column in student newspapers at Jacksonville University and the University of North Florida. Then I included as well miscellaneous writings by each of us, along with family photos scattered throughout.

I had intended to publish a full collection of Rose's poetry. (I may still do so.) I guess I ran out of steam. The same problem confronted me with the poems that I had faced with the novel—what was the final version she intended?

Undoubtedly, these publishing ventures were invaluable tools for recovering from the loss of Rose. As long as I was dealing on an almost daily basis with her writings, she was still there. I did one other thing that expedited my grief process.

On our first wedding anniversary after her death, I read for the first time all the letters she had written to me and I had written to her during our "courtship." There weren't a large number. Once we had discovered the depth of our love for each other, we were seldom apart. However, there were significant disclosures that, after more than forty-four years, seemed fresh and new. I repeated this exercise recently on what would have been our 62nd wedding anniversary. My current dilemma is, what shall I do with them now?

Male-Female Relationships

Until Rose's death, I'd never thought much about male-female relationships. Rose had made me a feminist (and I'm thankful for that). I had always had good friends who were female. In fact, that was my initial relationship with Rose. Before she died, Rose had made it clear to me that she was supportive of my finding another "significant other."

After her death, I made the decision that my most important agenda would be to learn how to live a fulfilling life as a single person. I had never really been an adult single. I lived with college and law school roommates until Rose and I were married. Now I was launched into, for me, uncharted territory. When I was a young teenager, there had been workshops on "boy-girl relationships." What I needed was a crash course for someone in his 60s.

During the early months of my "singleness," although I never had any romantic feelings for anyone, I had numerous significant friendships with women—some I had known for many years and some, new acquaintances. I enjoyed those friendships and those occasions for being together, but I never had what I considered a "date." In two instances, though, my friendship was misinterpreted as something more than that, and I found myself in extremely awkward situations. What I learned, the hard way, was this--to clarify my intentions early on so that there would be no misunderstanding interfering with potential friendships.

After nearly twenty years of singleness, I am content with my life. I've said that I'm open to being "struck by lightning," or being "swept off my feet" unexpectedly by a relationship. However, short of such an occurrence, I expect to remain single for the rest of my life.

(Whew, I'm glad that's said, and I can move on with this memoir.)

Memorial Presbyterian Church

In the fall of 2001, I had an "aha" moment. Although I had been a Methodist all my life (and generations before) and was even an ordained one, I was retired now and could go to whatever church suited me—or none at all. I emailed my pastor at Palm Coast (that was his preferred medium of communication) and told him that I planned to go elsewhere. I recited what I had come to realize were necessary aspects of a church experience for me, and stated that I hoped to find those elsewhere. I confessed that complete lack of pastoral care during the years of Rose's struggle contributed to that decision but insisted that it was not the primary reason. He replied that he'd like to talk to me about my decision but never made any effort to do so.

I don't know why I chose to visit Memorial Presbyterian Church in downtown St. Augustine, twenty-four miles away. Although I was familiar with many Presbyterian churches in that Presbytery and had even preached in several during my earlier tenure in Jacksonville, I knew almost nothing about Memorial. Rose and I had attended a Christmas Messiah presentation by the St. Augustine Community Chorus there on one or two occasions, so I knew the cathedral-like sanctuary. I also knew that the Chorus director was also the Memorial organist and choir director. That's all. If I believed that sort of thing (I don't), I would say God led me there.

My first Sunday, I completed a visitor's card as I had done at other churches when we moved back to Florida. I think I checked "please call," but didn't really expect to hear from anyone. Lo and behold, on Monday I had a call from John Hunter, the pastor. I had lost all my inhibitions at this point in my life, so I told him my whole story. I made it clear that I was cautious and didn't want to find myself in another church where I couldn't be myself. He asked what those "necessary aspects of a church experience for me" were. He listened to my list, one by one, and gave me an honest answer about each. It sounded like a fit, so I returned.

What hooked me, though, was an adult education experience I had early on. I saw in the church bulletin that Sheryl Aycock Anderson was leading a grief support group for five weeks on Sunday mornings. I had known Sheryl slightly during my earlier tenure in Jacksonville and thought that such a group experience might be helpful to me in adjusting to my new reality. It was, significantly so.

Sometime early in 2002, I "cast my lot" with that congregation. Since United Methodist ministers don't join local congregations (my membership is in the Virginia Conference, from which I retired), John found some way to categorize my relationship "decently and in good order." That congregation has been my church "family" ever since.

I love the music there, most of the time. I sang in the choir almost from the beginning until my vocal cord cancer and treatment made that no longer possible. The organ is spectacular and can send chills up my spine.

 I love the intellectual life of the church, especially its commitment to adult education. As one friend put it, "You don't have to check your brain when you come in the door." I've found a weekly educational offering that has continued to challenge me to grow. I've often taught short-term classes and continue to enjoy that experience on occasion.

I marvel at the breadth of the church's mission outreach, continuing to believe, as Emil Brunner put it, "The church exists by mission as a fire exists by burning." I served many years on the mission outreach committee and continue to be involved in some of its projects. For many years I coordinated the Food 4 Kids Project, providing weekend backpacks of food for 250 kids in need. I continue as an occasional volunteer in that program as well as Dining with Dignity, our monthly dinner for homeless persons.

I love the people, though, most of all. From the very beginning, I have experienced a deep, genuine caring among the members of the congregation. I miss being with them when I'm absent. Throughout my eighteen years there, I have been a part of many different programs and activities, enabling me to know dozens of people. They have enriched my life, even those with whom I have significant differences. Despite my appreciation for these affirming relationships, I long for greater racial and economic diversity.

Church Committee on Racial Reconciliation

Early in 2010, I joined an effort at the church initiated by Dick Rettig, a mostly retired social scientist. Authorized by the Session, our goal was to lead the congregation in a process aimed at racial reconciliation in the St. Augustine community. I'm not sure about the others on the Committee, but I had been inspired by earlier action taken by our neighbor, First United Methodist Church.

In 1964, First Methodist had denied entrance to local black citizens. When they had tried to enter anyway, they were arrested. The "kneel in" had been part of a city-wide protest in

St. Augustine over a period of several months. In 2004, the congregation had invited those same activists to a service of reconciliation, offering a public apology for their previous action.

I wanted to know what Memorial had been doing during that period. "Might we want to take similar action?" I asked. I began my search by reading University of Florida Professor David Colburn's history *Racial Change and Community Crisis: St. Augustine, Florida, 1877-1980*. In his account, I read that, at Memorial, the ushers had turned civil rights activists away without the knowledge of the pastor. When he learned about their action, the pastor had insisted that, in the future, all should be welcomed. In talking to church members who were active in 1964, they either denied his account or had no memory of the incident.

While that incident remains cloudy, I do know definitively about racist action by the Session in 1960. I've seen a copy of their "Statement to the Congregation" declaring that "the integration of white and negro races will not promote unity, and if allowed to become a part of the program…will effectually destroy all social and fellowship activity in the church." Further, they discontinued their subscription to the denominational publication and participation in the Synod's integrated conference-camp program for young people. They also ordered a review of all denominational literature "ascertaining whether [it] is objectionable in that it promotes integration of white and negro races." (After writing this, I have learned that some question that the Session really adopted this statement, although it appears to be clearly Session action on its face.)

I don't recall why our Committee ceased to function. Could it be that we were getting too close to "where the bodies were buried?" I know no serious efforts directed at racial reconciliation since then, although there have been initiatives to further interracial cooperation.

St. Augustine has an indefensible history of racial discrimination and injustice. I see no path to reconciliation until the white churches and community acknowledge with regret our past injustice.

Seekers

Since 2007, Seekers has been a central part of my life. It all began following a ten-week course taught by Mattie Hart and me. We had been discussing Marcus Borg's *The Heart of Christianity*, and some participants wanted to continue such discussions at a time other than Sunday morning. Almost every Sunday night since then, twenty or so of us have gathered for an hour and a half to discuss a book we've selected by popular vote. Discussion leaders rotate on a volunteer basis; I coordinate our efforts. We've read forty-eight books and watched four DVD series in our thirteen years together. Several have focused on racism, most notably *We Were Eight Years In Power*, by Ta-Nehisi Coates. Our current selection is Jon Meacham's *The Soul of America: The Battle for Our Better Angels*.

Feeding Homeless People.

In 2008, the Outreach Committee at the church asked me to design a series of four Wednesday night dinner programs on Homelessness. I was surprised at the size of the response, with more than 90 attendees each night. The first night, Renee

Morris, director of St. Francis House, our local shelter, came with four homeless persons to share what it is like to be homeless in St. Augustine. Because of the welcome they received, the homeless persons, sometimes joined by others, continued to attend the Wednesday night dinner programs, even after the four-week series was over.

Some members of the congregation began to feel uncomfortable about their presence. One young parent complained that a homeless person sat down next to her young son, and it was frightening to him. A staff member complained that she arrived at the church the next day to find a homeless person sleeping outside a church door. Of course, there were complaints about odors and sanitation.

When as many as 20 persons began attending regularly, the church leadership (independent of Kathy Vande Berg, the Outreach chair, or me) decided that our homeless guests would be asked not to attend. They were to be told when they showed up at the door that they were no longer welcome to come in. When we heard this was to happen, Kathy and I decided to intercept those we had come to know outside in the courtyard to inform them of what had been decided and to offer our apologies. It was one of the worst experiences of my life. Looking back now, I don't know why I did not leave the church.

Despite this incident, the Outreach Committee continued to reach out to the homeless community. A monthly dinner just for homeless persons, inviting any and all to come for a special meal, was instituted.

I remember an occasion, on a cold Friday night, when I was approached by one of our guests, letting me know that another guest had no coat. She asked if we had any coats available. After checking with others, I let her know that, regretfully, we did not. As they were leaving the dinner, I discovered that the homeless person seeking our help had given her own coat to the one in need.

Why did I not offer my coat to the one without? I had other coats at home, or could have bought another. From one we were trying to help that night, I learned a profound lesson about caring.

Although our church has continued to make efforts to serve the homeless population in St. Augustine, our commitment has been limited. I see the moment in 2008 when we turned folks away from our weekly dinner as a watershed moment. What might have happened to us and our guests if we had swung our doors open wide?

Methodist Federation for Social Action, Again

The United Methodist Church has a peculiar practice. A minister, after retirement, continues to be a member of the annual conference where that retirement occurred. Since I retired in Virginia, I will always be a member of the Virginia Conference. Although I've now lived in Florida for twenty-three years (this time), I have no relationship with the Florida Conference.

By 2004, though, I decided to become active again in the Florida Chapter of Methodist Federation for Social Action, an unofficial body of progressives. I took on the jobs of Treasurer and Membership Chair. After several years in those roles, I've moved on.

I miss my relationships in the United Methodist connection and my role as a social activist in the denomination. When I stepped back from that involvement, it was partly because I thought the younger clergy had become too "timid," afraid to take risks. I understood their caution, having been there myself--where my job, my home, my family could be in jeopardy. I understood, too, that my actions now were risk-free.

I view the younger clergy differently now. They seem to have lost their timidity, if that's what it was. They are taking huge risks, and they seem to be bringing the rest of the church with them in many instances. I applaud their courage and their commitment.

Travel

Travel was on our agenda when Rose and I retired early. Because of her battle with cancer, that plan was revised. Even when she was well enough to travel, she discovered that her goals had changed. She wanted to be at home, writing and nurturing friendships and family relationships.

Six months after her death, though, I took my first big trip— alone, to an Elderhostel in Northern Arizona, with a side trip to visit friends in Phoenix. Since I am an extrovert, I seldom feel alone, especially in travel groups like Elderhostel that cultivate community.

Since then, I have traveled overseas to the Galapagos Islands off the coast of Ecuador; gone on a safari to South Africa,

Botswana, Zimbabwe, Namibia, and Zambia; cruised on the Nile and traveled in Egypt and Jordan; cruised on the Yangtze and traveled in China, Tibet, and Hong Kong; and toured Australia and New Zealand. I've joined Elderhostel (now called Road Scholar) for trips in the U.S.--to San Francisco, Vermont, the Florida Everglades, and Key West. Another travel highlight was an off-road, four-wheel driving excursion in Nevada, Northern Arizona, and Utah with longtime friend Charles Frazier.

Another special adventure was a "boys" trip to Arizona and southern Colorado, with just my sons and grandson. We visited, for the first time, a five-acre lot in a remote development in the Sangre de Cristo Mountains, about a hundred miles north of Santa Fe. Bryan inherited it when his Shearouse grandfather died. (Nobody else wanted it.) It's high up a mountain, with a spectacular view. Unfortunately, it has no water or electrical access nearer than a mile. It was a wonderful bonding experience, and, hopefully, we can do another like it, even over the "unfairness" objection of granddaughters.

Martin Luther King Holiday Breakfasts

Soon after moving to Memorial Presbyterian, I began attending the annual Martin Luther King Holiday Breakfast. Each one was different, but all were inspirational. There was a particular one, though, that I'll never forget. It was on the Monday before the inauguration of Barack Obama as President.

There was a jubilant spirit in the room unlike any I'd previously witnessed. The program began, as I recall, with the singing of "Lift Every Voice and Sing." I'd learned it as a teenager, all the verses, before I even knew it was the Negro National Anthem.

I'd sung it and heard it sung many times in my life, but I had never heard it sung with such emotion. When we were finished, there were tears flowing all around me. The same spirit permeated the march downtown from St. Paul AME Church (scene of earlier civil rights rallies) to the market on the square where slaves had sometimes been sold.

I began to realize on that special day what the election of our first black President meant to the black community long denied full citizenship. While they had not yet arrived, they had come a long way.

Crossing in St. Augustine

I had not intended to include this, but decided I must. In 2011, St. Augustine finally decided to make amends for its unjust treatment of civil rights activists. The City erected a monument at the site where Andrew Young and others had been badly injured by a white mob almost forty-seven years earlier while local police stood watching. At the time, Young was one of the top leaders in the Southern Christian Leadership Conference. Here is how I heard him tell the story on one of his visits to the city.

A grassroots civil rights protest movement had emerged in St. Augustine in 1964, led by local dentist Dr. Robert Hayling. It was making national news because of the violent treatment of protesters. SCLC feared the movement was getting out of hand and might jeopardize efforts to pass pending civil rights legislation. Young had been sent down "to calm the waters."

When he arrived, the nightly mass meeting at the church was already underway. He was escorted up front and invited to address the crowd. Before he knew what was happening, the nightly protest march to the Plaza was underway, and he was the leader. As they approached the intersection of King and St. George Streets, the attack occurred. It was an ugly scene, and he (and others) could have easily been killed.

Whenever I pass the monument today, I remember our history. Yes, I say, let us not forget our history, the good and the bad. The difference between this monument and Civil War monuments, though, is that this monument reminds us of our past injustice and elicits our repentance. Civil War monuments, on the other hand, remind us of our past injustice and glorify our efforts to preserve and protect an unjust system.

More Family Matters and the Big "C"

By 2006, I was traveling to Dalton each month for a three or four day stay, helping my mother and sister manage their affairs. They were able to live independently in a duplex home, with indoor connection, until 2009. Wonderful caregivers provided tender loving care after that, 24/7.

Meanwhile, in Ft. Lauderdale and Dallas, my sons and their families continued to flourish. I began to advance from kindergarten graduations to high school ones.

Although I was very active—playing tennis three days a week, walking on the beach most mornings, swimming laps most afternoons, in 2009, the Big "C" decided to pay me a visit. In my routine annual physical, my longtime (but still young) primary care physician, Michael Phillips, felt "something irregular" when doing a manual examination of my prostate. It was aggressive, high-grade prostate cancer. After forty-two daily radiation treatments and two years of hormone injections, I was cancer free (and still am).

Part XI   Westminster Woods on Julington Creek

In the summer of 2011, just as I was turning 76, I began to think seriously about moving to a continuing care retirement community. I was still active, in good health, and enjoying my beach life and frequent travel.

A tape had been playing in my head since 1989, though, placed there by my father-in-law. He and my mother-in-law had moved to Magnolia Manor, a continuing care retirement community, when he was 81, and she was 80. He had gone "kicking and screaming" because she had insisted. After they had moved, though, each time we visited, he would say, "You need to do this when you get older, and you need to do it sooner rather than later."

I began to pay attention to that advice. Then some friends, younger than I, announced they were moving to Glenmoor, a continuing care retirement community at World Golf Village. He was a cancer survivor, and although he was cancer free, they thought it prudent to be prepared for the future. Next, a couple I knew from choir told me they were moving to Westminster Woods on Julington Creek—into a brand-new villa still under construction. I began to think about how nice it would be not to care for a lawn, a pool, and perpetually deteriorating beachfront property.

With all these "signs" converging, I was soon in the marketing offices at Glenmoor, Westminster, and Penney Farms (another continuing care retirement community in the Jacksonville area).

Before the week was out, I had made my decision, and signed a contract to "purchase" the first villa to be completed in Southwood Village at Westminster. In another month or two, I had sold my house in Palm Coast. On November 3, 2011, I moved into Unit A, 19 Tulipwood Court, where I hope someday to die (but not for a while, yet).

I loved my 14+ years living on the beach in the Hammock in Flagler County (the longest time I ever lived in a house, other than the one I grew up in). The Hammock had been the frontier (home of moonshiners, I was told) and still felt wild. I grew to love my neighbors (most of them). I loved the closeness to nature, especially the sea turtles that nested on our coquina beach. I invested myself in our community. I was the Treasurer of the Civic Association, President of the Homeowners Association, a worker at the polls on election days, and active in efforts to preserve our environment, including frequent visits to County Commission meetings. But now it was time to move on.

More Travel

Just because I was now living in an "old folks home" was no reason to stop traveling. Family responsibilities and health issues curtailed my overseas travel for a time, but I never lost sight of the fact that there is still a big world out there to be explored. In 2015, I celebrated my 80th birthday with all of my family on a cruise circling the Hawaiian Islands. In 2017, I managed a 41-day, 4,865 mile road trip to various locations in the United States and Canada, visiting special sites like Crater Lake and Glacier Park I had missed on earlier trips.

I had planned (for the second time) a trip to Copper Canyon in Northern Mexico with my friend Charles Frazier, but he died in

2014 before we could make our trip. When I heard that a neighbor in my community, Judy Ratcliffe, was planning to go there in 2016, I invited myself to join the tour. This time (my third attempt), the tour was canceled due to unrest in that part of Mexico. (Yes, I got the message. I'm not supposed to go to Copper Canyon.) Since we were "psyched" for a trip, Judy and I went instead on a Road Scholar excursion to Costa Rica in 2018.

A trip with campus minister friends to the Canadian Maritimes this August was cancelled because of the Covid-19 pandemic, so I'm sidelined for the moment. However, I have not yet given up on my travel dreams. Although I've now visited all fifty states and all the continents except Antarctica, there's still a lot of world out there, waiting for my visit. Maybe Ireland and an East Africa safari next?

Life at Westminster

I love my life at Westminster. During the pandemic, I've become acutely aware of how fortunate I am to be surrounded by all the natural beauty of our 90-acre campus. On my extended daily walks, I see lots of water fowl in our Turtle Lake and along Julington Creek (half a mile wide, much more than a creek). I admire the majesty of our towering oaks, pines, and magnolias. I stop to smell the flowers.

As I pass neighbors along our walkways, I'm able to call them by name and engage with many of them about their lives. It's like living in a small town, surrounded by people who know and care about you. (Yes, sometimes maybe even know too much about you.)

I've been active, as you might expect, in campus life and numerous activities. For three years, I was a member of the Residents' Council, more than two years as President. I recently resigned my membership in the Employee Scholarship Committee after many years of service. I'll always be active since I've never learned to say "no" to an invitation to be part of something.

Although I gave up tennis, I play pickleball now, as well as bocce and horseshoes, when available. I play bridge at least twice each month. I try to stay fit with a fitness class and workouts in our fitness center. I keep saying I'm going to resume my daily swims; maybe I will.

I cook most of my own meals, but enjoy knowing I can go to our dining hall whenever I choose. I continue to be engaged extensively in life in St. Augustine, although I've been saying for five years that I am going to center my life on campus, anticipating the day I will no longer be able to drive. My life here is good.

The Big "C" Again—and Again

Just before Thanksgiving in 2013, the Big "C" struck again. This time, it was a squamous cell cancer on my right vocal cord. Laser surgery took care of it, leaving me with a diminished voice but still able to speak and sing. The hardest part of the experience was remaining silent for several days following the surgery. Picture me carrying an erasable white board around stating, "Vocal cord surgery. Can't talk." When I would hold it up, explaining my silence, people would frequently want to write a reply on my board. So I had to add: "But I can still hear."

With frequent checkups, I felt assured I was cancer-free. However, just before the fifth anniversary of the first occurrence, another squamous cell cancer was detected—and in the very same location. This time, the treatment regimen was twenty-eight daily radiation treatments. Again, I appear to be cancer-free, most recently confirmed at Mayo on July 22.

When Rose had breast cancer treatments, one of the hardest losses she experienced was the loss of her ash blond hair. It had always been her distinctive feature. I remember watching her cry the day it began to fall out in clumps, the only tears I saw her shed during her entire cancer ordeal.

My vanity had always been centered in my speaking voice. I was sure the loss of its quality would be a huge blow to my self-identity. However, that has not been the case. I am grateful just to be able to speak understandably, even though raspy. A much larger deprivation has been the loss of my ability to sing. Although my singing voice was merely mediocre, I found great pleasure in singing with the St. Augustine Community Chorus and the Memorial Church Choir for many years. I am no longer able to do that.

Lots of Reunions

As you've probably noted, I like to keep up with people from various stages of my life, beginning with high school. Since I don't live in Dalton where I graduated, I have not usually been a planner of those reunions but am frequently asked to be a speaker. At our 50th in 2003, I published an anniversary edition of our high school newspaper, The Dalton Hi Light, which I had edited. To gather news, I crafted a questionnaire and used some of the responses to write a composite speech for the occasion.

My last "appearance" was at our 65th in 2018, when I challenged those of us who are still left to "make a plan for the rest of our lives."

I also celebrated the 50th anniversary of my law school graduation with the handful of us who had graduated in August 1959. I joined another small group to celebrate the 50th anniversary of my seminary graduation in 2014.

The most fun, though, has been the reunions of the many friends made at Camp Glisson in the 50s and 60s. Our latest one was in 2013. The older I get, the more nostalgic I become for "those good old days."

I've been trying for years to generate a reunion of all my first cousins. I think I counted twenty-two still living when my sister died. So far I've been unsuccessful. That dream may have to wait until another life.

Lunch at the South Beach Grill

Betty Meers, Jo Brooke, and Theresa Dove Waters had been colleagues and friends of my late wife Rose at the University of North Florida. When we get together, we are a strange foursome. Theresa and I are both United Methodist ministers, now retired. Betty is a devout Roman Catholic, and Jo is, well I'm not sure. All of us are liberal Democrats. Oh, I failed to mention that Theresa is black, while the other three of us are white. And, of course, they're female and I'm male. I think what binds us together is that we all loved Rose.

We had been getting together for lunch three or four times a year ever since Theresa retired from a teaching position and a ministerial appointment in Georgia, sometime in the fall of 2011, I think. When she decided to make her retirement home in Palm Coast, I was getting ready to move from there to Westminster Woods, just south of Jacksonville. I introduced her to my realtor and neighbor, Karen Joyce, who helped her find a new home.

Betty and Jo are longtime Jacksonville residents. We usually drove together to meet Theresa halfway. On this particular day, the three of us showed up at South Beach Grill in Crescent Beach several minutes early, as we usually did. Theresa was driving from Palm Coast and was running late, as she often did. We had told the young woman at the reception desk that we were expecting "a friend" to meet us and asked her to direct Theresa to our table when she arrived.

We were sipping our iced tea and enjoying the ocean view from the second floor dining room when Theresa finally found us. She had arrived earlier and told the receptionist she was meeting friends. When the receptionist replied there was no one waiting, Theresa had proceeded to check out the two floors of dining anyway until she found us. Theresa was the only person of color in the restaurant, and all four of us were sure that the receptionist had assumed her "friends" must be black as well. Whenever we gathered there in the future, we made sure the staff knew the color of the persons waiting and the persons expected. It became a standing joke among us.

We seem to find it remarkably easy to talk about race with one another. We can even laugh about the fact that Betty, Jo, and I are usually early and Theresa is usually late—maybe a cultural difference? I feel free to share exactly how I feel about almost anything with them, and they seem to feel the same way. Such trust is rare, and I treasure our times together.

A Special Note About Betty

Betty is my go-to person when I need help, as I am for her. She picks me up after out-patient procedures when I need a driver; I do the same for her. As the Beatles have frequently reminded me, "I get by with a little help from my friends." Betty has been that special friend for years now. She is usually the one I call when I need to talk to someone.

We also have enjoyed the Jacksonville Symphony Coffee Concerts together for many seasons. I suggested the name for her dog Andy, and, in return, I get to be his sitter when Betty goes away. Her latest second-mile service for me was being my proofreader for this memoir. Thanks, Betty.

More Family Matters

In 2010, my mother celebrated her 100th birthday, with a son, a daughter, three sisters, multiple nieces, nephews, and their spouses, two special friends, and two caregivers present. She loved it! She lived two more years and died at home less than two weeks short of her 102nd birthday, with Helen and me at her bedside.

My sister Helen died in 2016, less than a week short of her 82nd birthday, with her faithful caregivers and me at her bedside. Although younger, I was always the big brother, primarily because she was born with spina bifida. She defied the odds and the doctors who expected her to live only six years. She refused to let her "handicap" define who she was and what she did. She donated her body to Emory University Medical School.

After Helen's death, my life changed considerably—no more monthly trips to Dalton. However, I continue to communicate weekly with the very special person who managed care for my mother and sister for many years, Freda Boring. She is still part of my family.

Granddaughter Samantha has graduated from Florida State University and has completed three years as a flight attendant with American Airlines (following in her mother's footsteps). Granddaughter Callie, after graduation from Florida State University, is in a graduate program at Florida Atlantic University to be a Guidance Counselor. Granddaughter Alaina completed a business degree at Tarrant County Community College and has been working in Jacksonville. At the beginning of July, though, she moved back to Dallas.

This would have been a big year of college graduation celebrations for me if Covid-19 had not intervened. Grandson Troy graduated from the University of Central Florida in May, virtually. Granddaughter Jessica will graduate virtually, too, from Florida State University on July 31. Granddaughter Julia expects to do the same in December, and Granddaughter Rebecca expects to graduate in December as well--from Fresno State College in California. At the moment, it looks doubtful that any will graduate "in person."

Yes, some of them have "significant others," but no spouses. I worry about their futures since the job market is so abysmal. I worry, too, about the world my generation is passing on.

Mark and Jill continue their stable lives in Ft. Lauderdale. Bryan and Laura were divorced last summer after thirty-one years of marriage. He remains in Naples, adjusting to his new status.

The Big "S"

I've always been told that the road to hell is paved with good intentions. I now know that to be the case. In 2012, when the first vaccine for shingles became available, I was an early recipient. However, when the new and better shingles vaccines became available, I had only "intended" to get inoculated. The "hell" arrived with a full-blown case of shingles in the fall of 2019. After a month of the experience, I was ready for anything that offered relief. Now, fully recovered and fully inoculated, I offer this free advice from one who knows: Don't just "intend." Do it.

XII   Ancestry

For at least fifty years, I've been pursuing my ancestry sporadically. My results were exponentially increased when I joined ancestry.com. I have now identified more than 127 ancestors by name. As you might have anticipated, 96% of my DNA is from the British Isles—England, Wales, Scotland, and Ireland. When son Mark saw the results, his comment was, "You're so white bread."

For some time, I've been interested in knowing what role my ancestors have played in the racism that has permeated our society for 400 years. I have been well aware that I am a beneficiary of white privilege, but I wanted to know just how. So I've been exploring. I'll share some of the results here.

My Ancestors and Indian Lands

I had always thought that my mother's father, Hilley Green Roach, had Indian blood. He had features remarkably similar to the Cherokee who had lived in Northwest Georgia where he grew up. So did two of his sisters I had met. But DNA doesn't lie. No Indian blood. His father had, I learned, been married to an Indian woman when he left to serve in the Confederate Army. However, she had deserted him during the war and was not the mother of my grandfather.

I had wondered as well about when and how my ancestors had acquired the lands they owned in Northwest Georgia, an area occupied by the Cherokee until their forcible removal between 1836 and 1839. I know at least one, Thomas J. Griffin (1817-1894), received a 160-acre lot in East Armuchee in Walker County in the land lottery that followed the removal of the Cherokee. I have not yet done the research needed to determine precisely how and when other Northwest Georgia ancestors acquired their land. I may need to leave that for another generation to pursue.

My Ancestors and Slave Ownership

I had wondered, too, about slave ownership. My impression had been that almost all my ancestors had very limited wealth, if any. Most seemed to be subsistence farmers. How could they have afforded to own slaves?

Surprise! When I checked 1840 census records, I identified at least eight of my ancestor families who owned slaves. They owned a total of thirty-nine slaves. Here is a list of those eight ancestor families, the location of their residence, and a listing of their slaves.

In Chattooga County, Georgia, southwest of Dalton, lived two slaveholding families. On the paternal side of my family were Williams Crook (1781-1858) and Sarah Evins (1791-1863). They owned seven slaves, two males (one under ten and one over 55) and five females (three under ten and two over 24). The Crooks moved to Dalton before the War and are buried in the same cemetery where my cremains will be interred. Their son, Leander, brother of my great-great-grandmother Mary Eliza Crook Thomason, was the elected representative to the Georgia legislature before the War, a Superior Court Judge, and a Major in the Confederate Army. He was killed in 1862 and is buried beside his parents.

Also in Chattooga County, but on the maternal side, were John Isham (1790-1847) and Samantha Henderson (1791-1847). They owned only one slave—a male over 24.

In Elbert County, in northeast Georgia, two paternal ancestor families were living. John Lawson Henton (1806-1857) and Elizabeth T. Hulme (1808-1883). Their slaves were two males (one under ten and another over 36) and a female over 24. Nearby were Elizabeth's parents, John Hulme (1773-1857) and Elizabeth Alexander (1779-1859). They owned six slaves, three males (one under ten and two over 24) and three females (two under ten and another over ten). The Hentons moved to Dalton after 1850.

One maternal ancestor family also lived in Elbert County— Thomas R. Pledger (1764-1846) and Nancy Leavister (1770-1843). They owned eight slaves, two males (one under ten and another over 36) and six females (three under ten, two over ten, and one over 24).

Nearby, in Franklin County, Georgia, lived a paternal ancestor family—Nancy A. Carruthers (1774-1862), widow of William Madison Thomas (1763-1835), living with her son Madison. She owned four slaves, two males (one under ten and another over 55) and two females (one under ten and one over 10).

In Laurens County, South Carolina, lived paternal ancestors Gideon Thomason (1783-1867) and Ellender Stuart (1782-1860). They owned eight slaves, five males (two under ten, three over ten) and three females (one under ten, one over ten, and one over 24). It is noteworthy that they are listed as charter members of Dials Methodist Church in Laurens County in 1813, along with nine other whites and two slaves. Circuit Rider Francis Asbury was the organizer of the congregation, and Gideon paid for one of the two acres of land on which the church building was erected.

Finally, in Iredell County, North Carolina, lived Esther Starrett (1771-1860), widow of Henry Dobson (1750-1834). She owned two slaves, both female (one under ten, one over 24). She had moved there from Northwest Georgia after Henry's death.

As I have read the listing of these enslaved human beings, unnamed and only identified by age categories, I have wondered about family separations that may lie behind these configurations. I've also wondered if any of the children listed were "fathered" by one of my ancestors, as was often true.

Since I am a direct descendant of these eight slaveholding families (and likely others I have been unable to identify), I am an inheritor of white privilege, a direct beneficiary of the fruits of slave labor. I say this, not to wallow in guilt or to characterize myself as a bad person, but simply to declare a fact about my personal history. I am still struggling to determine what that reality means for me.

My Ancestors and the Civil War

I had known that some of my ancestors had fought in the Civil War--in the Confederate Army, of course. I wanted to know more. Here is what I learned.

On the paternal side of my family, my great-grandfather, Leander Williams Thomason (1848-1929), was a member of the 1st Regiment of the South Carolina Infantry from August 12, 1864 until April 6, 1865. He apparently enlisted a week after his 16th birthday. My dad said that he had been wounded and, as a result, walked with a cane for the rest of his life.

On my maternal side, another great-grandfather, Joshua Adam Roach (1838-1924), was a member of the 19th Alabama Infantry. Since he was living in Tunnel Hill in Whitfield County, I am not sure why he enlisted in Alabama. Among other battles (including Shiloh), he fought in the Battle of Chickamauga, only a few miles from his home. His handwritten account of that day's fighting is in the archives in Dalton.

Here's a good story about his account of the battle. It was "discovered" in 2013 when Steve Hall, another descendant of Joshua, was doing research for the 150th commemoration of Civil War events in and around Dalton. After reading it, he decided to go to the Chickamauga National Battlefield Park and try to follow the battle. He made his trek there on the very day of the battle (September 19), exactly 150 years later. When he reached the battle line, he saw that someone else was already there. In conversation, he learned that the other visitor was from Indiana, doing the very same thing he was doing. However, the other visitor's ancestor had been on the other side. Steve described the experience as "spooky."

Another ancestor who fought in the War was Andrew Jackson Warnock (1815-1868), my great-great-grandfather. He was apparently in the same regiment as Joshua, surprisingly, an Alabama regiment. He lived in East Armuchee, Walker County, Georgia, just west of Whitfield County. His daughter, Mary Parmelia (1852-1886), after the War, married another of my ancestors who fought in the War, William Henry Griffin.

William Henry Griffin (1846-1936), another maternal great-grandfather, was also from East Armuchee. He was in the 39th Georgia Infantry.

Now here's a really good story. It is not commonly known that the South had a substantial number of citizens who were opposed to secession and never supported the Confederacy. Walker and Chattooga counties (where some of my ancestors lived) opposed secession. However, after the state legislature voted in favor of secession, most of the citizens supported the decision, but not all.

Thomas J. Griffin (1817-1894), father of William Henry, was pro-Union. His oldest son, Needham, had enlisted in the Confederate army in 1862, though, maybe at the same time as William Henry, his younger brother. Although they were in the same regiment, apparently they were in different companies. They were both captured at the Battle of Vicksburg, but were later paroled after signing an Oath of Allegiance. In 1864, Thomas left Georgia to work on the Union railroad in Nashville, then in Union hands, assisting Needham (declared AWOL) to join him there. William Henry continued his service in the Confederate army until the end of the War.

Since learning about this family division, I've wondered how it played out after the War. Thomas, Needham, and William Henry all came home to Walker County to live and rear their families.

If I were to write a historical novel, I would try to create the post-war story of these three Griffins. (No, I don't plan to write one unless there's another pandemic.)

Lynching

As I learned more about the atrocities committed against blacks after the War, I wanted to know more about where those acts took place and the people who perpetrated them.

At the beginning of November, 2019, I traveled to Montgomery, Alabama, to meet old friends from the 50s—Bill Cole from Charlotte, North Carolina, Barrett and Barbara Talley Smith from Pine Mountain, Georgia, and Rhoda and Doug Joyner, from Decatur, Georgia. We had come to see the sites that memorialize more than 4,400 African Americans who were lynched across 20 states between the end of Reconstruction in 1877 and 1950.

At the National Memorial for Peace and Justice, 800 six-foot monuments are displayed. Each one represents a county in the United States where a racial terror lynching took place. The name of each victim and the date of the lynching are engraved on the monument. To walk among those memorials takes your breath away.

I immediately began searching for Whitfield County, Georgia, where my roots are. Sometime during the last ten years, while at the beauty shop in Dalton with my sister, I had overheard a conversation about a lynching in Dalton. The two conversers mentioned a participant whose name I recognized, the father of one of my grade school classmates. Curious, I had intended to pursue the shocking information I had never before heard as a child growing up there.

When I found the Whitfield County monument, the reality of what it documented sent shivers up my spine. There were five names listed. The first four men were lynched between 1888 and 1892. The fifth, though, was lynched on September 6, 1936, during my lifetime (I was a year old.) His name was A. L. McCamy. He was 21-years-old, and had been accused of an attempted attack on a white woman. According to a contemporaneous newspaper account (from Detroit, not Dalton), a mob of 150 men had stormed the local jail, seized Mr. McCamy, and spirited him away. His body was found four hours later on a roadside beneath a tree from which he had been hanged.

In 1936, at the time of the lynching, my dad and his older brother Clarence were operating a single counter café just a block north of the jail. I'm sure he knew about the incident, although he never mentioned it. I can't imagine that he would have been a part of the mob, but he must have known some, probably most, of the perpetrators. I wish he were still alive so I could ask him about it.

Part XIII   The Future

Reparations, Monuments, and Systemic Racism

I mention the three topics above because they have been the focus of much conversation during recent weeks. There are many other topics as well that will demand our attention if we are to make progress in forging a non-racist society.

When the topic of reparations is introduced, the first response of white folks like me is, "I didn't own slaves. Why should reparations be expected from me?" Another common response, directed to people of color, is: "You weren't a slave. Why should you benefit because somebody else, even if your ancestor, was enslaved?" While I do not have an answer to propose for these vexing questions, I am nevertheless convinced that our society must find some way to correct the imbalance that has ensued from 400 years of racial oppression. I fully support the concept of reparations; I just don't know what form such redress should take. I place this topic high on the agenda for the future.

Confederate monuments is another topic in daily headlines. I've already declared my perspective on the removal of monuments that glorify the Confederacy. Because descendants of former slaves are painfully reminded daily of the War to preserve slavery and "the Southern way of life" by such monuments, they should be removed from prominent public display. As a society, we have already caused enough pain to people of color; let's not add more.

As difficult as these topics are, systemic racism is exponentially more difficult. It suggests that our whole society is infected with racism and our only remedy is a complete overhaul of the system. Of course, that is precisely our reality. While I do not have the prescription to "fix it," I do believe that we should be pursuing a systemic solution. I am encouraged that, at last, we appear to be acknowledging the severity of our disease and our need for a radical cure.

Some Books About Race That Have Changed My Life

Stride Toward Freedom: The Montgomery Story (1956), by Martin Luther King, Jr., is the story of the Montgomery Bus Boycott of 1955-56. It, more than any other book, provided my earliest understanding of the depths of racism and the crucial importance of nonviolent confrontation in the struggle to overcome it.

Two other King books, *Strength to Love* (1963), sermons about race, and *Why We Can't Wait* (1964), about the 1963 Birmingham campaign, enabled me to comprehend the urgency of the movement for racial justice.

Invisible Man (1952), by Ralph Ellison, *Black Like Me* (1961), by John Howard Griffin, and *I Know Why the Caged Bird Sings* (1969), by Maya Angelou, helped me "feel" more deeply what living life as a black person in America is like.

The Autobiography of Malcolm X (1965), with Alex Haley, and *The Fire Next Time* (1963), by James Baldwin, while more strident, provided me necessary alternative views to the mainline civil rights perspective.

Numerous novels have helped to shape my emotional understanding, especially those by Zora Neal Hurston, Toni Morrison, Alice Walker, and James Baldwin.

These books about the civil rights movement have been particularly helpful—Taylor Branch's account of the King years, *Parting the Waters: America in the King Years, 1954-63* (1988) and John Lewis's memoir, *Walking with the Wind: A Memoir of the Movement* (1999).

Two books that have transformed my understanding of how racism functions in the criminal justice system are *Just Mercy: A Story of Justice and Redemption* (2014), by Brian Stevenson, and *The New Jim Crow: Mass Incarceration in the Age of Colorblindness* (2010), by Michelle Alexander.

More recent books have shaped my thinking as well, particularly *We Were Eight Years in Power* (2017), by Ta-Nehisi Coates, and *White Fragility: Why It's So Hard for White People to Talk About Racism* (2018), by Robin DiAngelo, which I'm currently reading.

I rejoice that so much good material is becoming available because of the current flood of concern about our racist history and our urgent need to address constructively the gaping wound at the heart of our society. I expect to continue reading constantly in order to remain relevant in the discussions to come.

Planning My Future

As you would expect, I have a plan for the future. No timeline, but, whenever my body has had enough, here's my plan. I have an already-paid-for contract with the Neptune Society for my cremation. It even includes insurance to pay for the shipment of my body back from anywhere in the world, just in case I'm on some exotic island when it happens. (I just realized. I don't know whether or not that includes outer space. I should have checked.)

My cremains are to be buried in the Thomason Family plot in West Hill Cemetery in Dalton, beside those of Rose, my sister Helen, and my parents. I plan to have a simple tombstone matching the others, but I still need to arrange for that (putting it on my to-do list).

I want to have my memorial service at Westminster Woods, with plenty of food and drink either before or after. I have asked three clergy women to do the service (all considerably younger than me, hoping they'll still be around). They are Carol Armstrong-Moore, Martha Rutland-Wallis, and Charlene Kammerer. I don't know what my theology or liturgical taste will be by that time (it seems to change daily), but I trust them to "do the right thing." I still don't know what I want to do about music, which has been an important part of my life. I'll have to think about that for a while longer. I may write my own obituary (since no one else knows all the details of my life), or I may just leave that for Mark and Bryan to figure out.

My financial affairs are in order, of course. I have arranged to donate 20% of whatever I have left to "charities" I currently support, making gifts directly from my IRAs. I revise that list frequently, but I want to continue to "make a difference" with my money after I die. Giving to others from my financial resources has been one of the joys of my life. The other 80% I'm leaving for my family, as my parents did for me.

My father-in-law Sam taught me many things, one of them being how to die. (So did Rose, mainly by her courageous example.) I remember our last visit with Sam. He had been in an Americus hospital for several days, fighting pneumonia. He wanted us to get his music from his villa, especially the pieces he had copied from a recording to be played at his memorial service. It was Sunday, four days before his death on Thursday. As we were leaving to return to Palm Coast for Rose's first chemotherapy session that week, he said to us, "I've lived a long, full life (he was about to turn 91), and I'm prepared to die. But in case I don't, will you take me to the Holy Land?"

That's how I want to be—ready to die, but with an agenda for the future if it doesn't happen right away.

One of my favorite quotes is from Dag Hammarskjold, the late Secretary General of the United Nations. It has concluded my ministry in five places; let it conclude my life.

"For all that has been, thanks. To all that shall be, yes!"

Afterword

Writing this memoir has been an amazing journey. When I began writing on June 1, I had no idea I would have this much to say. Recalling the obvious landmarks of my life frequently led me to remember other, less dramatic incidents that I had not thought about since they originally happened. Those incidents sometimes became significant in understanding my life story.

As I wrote, I also began to see some of the events of my past in a new light. As my understanding of racism grew, my self-understanding did, too. Consequently, the writing has been an emotional journey. I think I am a better person because of it.

I have strived to be completely honest in telling my story. I am self-aware enough to know that I have not always been able to do that. I hope you'll be able to forgive me for those times I have not lived up to my own standards.

I'm sure I have made factual errors and that my memories have not always corresponded precisely with what others who were present remember. When Rose was writing her memoir, she did not always remember events we had both experienced in the same way that I did. If you were there and remember something differently, let me acknowledge in advance that you may be right. My mind, I'm convinced, sometimes alters my memory to make it more compatible with my desired version.

Writing this life story has not always been a pleasant experience. I have lost a lot of sleep during the seven weeks I have labored over it. Once you open the spigot of memory, it's difficult to turn off the flow. Had I not lain awake nights reliving certain events, my account would have been less true.

The pandemic is far from over, though, so I will have plenty of time to sleep.

If you are still reading this, you must have found something about my life experience that resonates with yours. I hope so. I was taught growing up that it's not polite to talk about oneself. However, I've discovered over the years that sharing what has shaped me, what I value, what matters to me, is the only personal truth I have to offer.

While writing this Afterword, I learned of the death of civil rights icon John Lewis. His life has inspired me. I've tried to follow his advice: "If you see something that is not right, not fair, not just, you have a moral obligation to do something about it." Sometimes I've managed to do so.

Thank you for listening.

Robert Troy Thomason
July 18, 2020

About the Author

Robert Thomason spent his forty-year career as a campus minister in Georgia, Florida, and Virginia. A son of the South with deep generational roots in the "Southern way of life," his passion for justice has led him to challenge the ways of his homeland and its institutions. He was married for forty-two years to his soulmate Rose Shearouse, a leader in the church's women's movement, until her death in 2001. They are the parents of two sons, a grandson, and six granddaughters. A young 85, he lives a very active life in a continuing care retirement community at Westminster Woods on Julington Creek in St. Johns, Florida.